Dan
Harrison

with Maria Henderson

INTERVARSITY PRESS
DOWNERS GROVE, ILLINOIS 60515

1991

InterVarsity Press is the book-publishing division of InterVarsity Christian Fellowship, a student movement active on campus at hundreds of universities, colleges and schools of nursing in the United States of America, and a member movement of the International Fellowship of Evangelical Students. For information about local and regional activities, write Public Relations Dept., InterVarsity Christian Fellowship, 6400 Schroeder Rd., P.O. Box 7895, Madison, WI 53707-7895.

All Scripture quotations, unless otherwise indicated, are from the Holy Bible, New International Version. Copyright © 1973, 1978, International Bible Society. Used by permission of Zondervan Bible Publishers.

Maps on pages 48 and 49 used by permission of Luis Bush.

ISBN 0-87784-1334-9

Printed in the United States of America ⊗

Library of Congress Cataloging-in-Publication Data

Harrison, Dan, 1941-
   Hope for the world/by Dan Harrison, Maria Henderson.
     p.   cm.
   ISBN 0-8308-1334-9
   1. Hope—Religious aspects—Christianity.   I. Henderson, Maria.
II. Title.
BV4638.H33   1991
234'.2—dc20   *91-15202*
                                                                 CIP

15	14	13	12	11	10	9	8	7	6	5	4	3	2	1
03	02	01	00	99	98	97	96	95	94	93	92	91		

Introduction

What is Urbana?

It is the thrill of nearly 20,000 voices raised together in worship and song. It is the hushed attention of those 20,000 catching a new vision of God's work in the world through a video presentation or a speaker's challenge. Urbana is the special excitement of thousands of young people earnestly seeking to understand God's will for their lives. Urbana is many things that cannot be put into a book, but most of all, Urbana 90 was about hope. This book is intended to share something of the event with those who weren't able to attend the convention, as well as to refresh the memories of those who attended.

Urbana 90 was the sixteenth student mission convention sponsored by InterVarsity Christian Fellowship in Canada and the United States, following the tradition begun in 1946 when 545 delegates gathered in Toronto. At the conclusion of that first convention, Stacey Woods, founder of InterVarsity in North America, prayed that God would not only raise up missionaries from that gathering, but a true missionary movement. Urbana 90 was over 19,000 students, hundreds of InterVarsity staff, 1750 missionaries (representing over 200 agencies and more than 50 seminaries and Bible institutes), and 2,000 student Bible study leaders. Urbana is the university of world missions, offering hundreds of seminars and ministry models led by prominent leaders in a variety of fields related to the task of world mission and preparation for service.

Urbana is the 140,000 people around the globe who have attended an Urbana convention and have put the convictions gained there into action. Perhaps as many as 30 to 40 per cent of them have been called to crosscultural missionary service.

Urbana has also become an international movement as God has raised up similar conventions for students in fifteen countries around the world. During Urbana 90, delegates participated in a telephone link-up with thousands of students attending Mission 90 in Mexico City.

Urbana is Paul Leary, who was a student at Urbana 79, experienced crosscultural training through InterVarsity Missions, served on InterVarsity staff and is now going to Africa as a missionary, along with a team of friends and colleagues from his student days. During his ten years on staff, Paul has seen more than one hundred of his students become missionaries.

Urbana is Stacey Chapman, who grew up in the projects of Atlanta, and who was part of a multiethnic mission team in the Soviet Union last year that was instrumental in leading more than thirteen Soviet students and three faculty to saving faith in Christ. Stacey is returning to the Soviet Union as a staff member on a pioneering team going to another Soviet university.

My road to Urbana began in 1964 with the commitment my wife and I made to God's work in the world when we joined Wycliffe Bible Translators.

In a sense I have been involved in missions all my life, having been born in China where my parents were missionaries for twenty-three years among the Tibetans. I had been to several Urbanas as a representative of Wycliffe Bible Translators and had seen the potential impact. During those five days in 1984, our team interviewed 3,000 prospective Bible translators.

As I was considering the opportunity to serve as director of Urbana and InterVarsity Missions, I wondered why so many young people commit themselves to mission at Urbana, and what happens to them after they make those decisions. What I've learned about the young people who come to Urbana and their continuing commitment to mission has only reinforced my understanding of the tremendous impact the conventions have. We studied the delegates who came to Urbana 87 and found that 97 per cent attend church at least once a week. Two-thirds had witnessed to someone within a month of Urbana, and 45 per cent could name a person they had led to faith in the Lord Jesus. One-third had been on a crosscultural mission trip of a month or more.

Interestingly enough, two-thirds of those who came to Urbana 87 did not come because it was a missions convention and/or did not really even understand world missions. They came because they are committed to Christ. Consequently, many were open to the challenge of the Great Commission, which gives every believer the responsibility and privilege of being involved in world mission: "Go therefore and make disciples of all nations, baptizing them in the name of the Father and of the Son and of the Holy Spirit, teaching them to observe all that I have commanded you" (Mt 28:19-20).

What is the impact of Urbana over time? Do the thousands of students who make decisions follow through with them?

Do you remember a decision you made a year ago? How about four years ago? In 1988 we conducted a telephone poll of a random sample of delegates who had made a commitment to world mission at Urbana 84. What we found was astonishing:

43 per cent of them remembered their decision and had either begun to fulfill it or were still committed to doing so. One of the reasons these decisions were not forgotten is because of the InterVarsity Missions follow-up program, conducted in partnership with local churches, which provides resources to delegates for years after they attend an Urbana.

Planning for Urbana 90 began more than three years earlier, when we began to look at the world as it would be in 1990 and even more importantly as it might be in 1995 or 2005, when we expect that most of the delegates attending Urbana 90 will be ready to begin their missionary service. We looked at a world full of war and strife, struggling with poverty, injustice and environmental destruction, where thousands die each day without knowing the Savior. We determined to focus the convention on the theme of hope—Jesus Christ: Lord of the Universe, Hope of the World. In the face of the world's terrible need, there is no other hope, no other name by which we must be saved.

We wanted to portray hope in Jesus Christ for the Islamic world—not knowing that we would gather just two weeks before the outbreak of war in the Persian Gulf. We wanted students to grasp hope for the hungry of our world and recognize that they could make a difference—demonstrated as more than 19,000 people cooperated by skipping one meal and contributing to an offering that raised more than $300,000. We wanted to enable students to proclaim Christ effectively on their campuses in the midst of prevailing attitudes of relativism and the popular New Age movement, equipping them with solid understanding of the uniqueness of Christ. We wanted to proclaim hope for those without Christ, especially those immediately around the delegates as they returned to their campuses or workplaces.

We looked at the people who would be attending this Urbana, most of them members of what *Time* magazine has called the "twenty-something generation" of young people between the ages of 18 and 29. We were shocked by this student generation's need for a message of hope. One survey suggests that 85 per cent of the twenty-something generation do not believe it is possible to have a permanent marriage relationship—they have grown up in an era of high divorce rates and single-parent homes. Yet if you ask them what they want most, it's a committed marriage.

These are issues that confront Christians as much as non-Christians, and for many they seem an insurmountable barrier to participation in the Great Commission. "How can I do anything worthwhile in reaching the world for Christ when I'm so broken, when my background is so dysfunctional?" many students are asking. Others wonder whether the Bible, written so long ago to such different cultures, can speak to today's issues. We felt we could not call this generation to global mission without addressing their need for hope for their own personal healing and the reconciliation of broken relationships in their lives.

God honored himself in many ways through Urbana 90. Hundreds of people received prayer for their dysfunctional backgrounds. Hundreds of others experienced reconciliation with siblings, classmates or parents. Lots of young people experienced a clearer sense of who they are in Christ and were empowered to be salt and light in their present circumstances and to prepare to witness wherever Christ sends them. The commitments they made by filling out a World Evangelism Decision Card reflect the impact of the hope proclaimed at Urbana:

I received Jesus Christ as my Lord and Savior during Urbana 90 [122 respondents].

I unreservedly give myself to Jesus Christ as Lord of the universe. As an indication of my commitment, I will be actively involved in a church, on my campus and/or in the marketplace. Also I commit myself to studying Scripture, giving financially to and praying for God's work, and developing a lifestyle that reflects kingdom values [10,116 respondents].

I commit myself to begin more active involvement in global mission through a summer mission project, short-term service or career service [6,381 respondents].

I will become involved in global mission and commit myself to clarify how and when [4,475 respondents*].

Even more encouraging than these numbers are the letters I receive from students who want to share how God met them at Urbana. "I was seriously confronted with the sincerity of my personal pursuit of God. Was I willing to love people enough to respond to his call in loving my campus radically?" wrote a student from Occidental College. "I left Urbana believing that prayer is key to life and growth. I've begun to pray with people back at school, and it continues to amaze me how much prayer makes an immediate impact," wrote another from Stanford. These are young people taking seriously the challenge to love people for Jesus' sake, and their faithful efforts to live that dedication out today on their campuses gives me great hope for how God might use them and thousands of others like them all around the world in the years to come.

———————————

*Total number of delegates committing to decisions 3 and 4 was 9,192.

1

A Lasting Hope

Early Spring sat in a barren room, the flickering light of a candle illuminating the tears on her face. She held her paper near the candle, reading again the outpouring of her 13-year-old heart. "I have three wishes: I want my father to be well again. I want my family to be back together again. I want to go to school again."

Early Spring was one of the millions of victims of China's Cultural Revolution. Her father, a prominent politician, had fallen out of favor. He was living in the same concentration camp as Early Spring, but they could not see each other. In the course of the persecution he suffered, he had been injured. Early Spring's mother had denounced her husband in a desperate attempt to spare the rest of the family. Now she was in a psychiatric hospital and the rest of the family had been scattered across China. Early Spring's young life was shattered, but she clung to the hope that somehow those pieces could be put together again.

Ten years later, she told her story to an Australian who had come to teach in China. Mary Fisher listened as Early Spring told how each of her wishes had come true. Her father was well, her family back together, and she was studying at the university. But tears rolled down her face as she said, "Even though my wishes have been achieved, the last ten years have left me with nothing but a badly wounded heart."

Mary heard that heart's cry for a true hope, a hope that wouldn't disappoint, and she told Early Spring the story of how she had found that hope in Jesus Christ.

Mary had met Jesus Christ in 1972 while working as a journalist in one of Australia's larger cities. She was writing a story about a Christian group that had started a coffeehouse outreach to drug addicts. Mary couldn't understand why educated, professional people would spend their time caring for people who to her were very unattractive, and she couldn't explain the way their lives were being changed by the hope that they were experiencing. She didn't believe that God existed, but she finally prayed, "God, I don't believe you are there, but if you, are make yourself known."

God responded to her prayer.

During a number of years of living and working in China, Mary had many opportunities to share the hope within her with wounded people. But despite the fruitfulness of her ministry, there came a time when even she began to lose sight of that hope. Her father died, still a non-Christian. Her home church, her real family, split. Her Chinese friends faced insurmountable difficulties. One friend who desperately wanted a child discovered that his wife was probably sterile because of an earlier abortion. Another friend's work unit refused him permission to marry the person he wanted to marry. Mary's best friend, a writer, had not been allowed to write for years because some of his writings spoke of the gospel.

Mary's prayers about these problems remained unanswered. Finally she wrote to one of her former professors, Dr. Robert Mulholland, and explained, "While in my head I believe it all, in my heart it's like God has wound up the clock and walked away."

Dr. Mulholland wrote back a long letter in which he sympathized with all the suffering she had experienced in her own life and through her relationships with others in pain. Then he reminded her of the Bible's story about human suffering and pain, how the world was created and it was very good, but men and women rebelled against God and sin entered this perfect world. That catastrophe, he wrote, affects us to this day.

That, however, is only the beginning of the story. The New Testament reveals God's solution to that disaster. It was Peter who first acknowledged that Jesus was indeed the Christ, the Messiah, the one God had sent to be our Savior. But when Jesus explained that he was on his way to suffer and die on the cross, Peter argued with him—"Never, Lord!" However, Jesus said to his disciples then and says to his followers today, "As the Father has sent me, so send I you." "Salvation," wrote Dr. Mulholland, "is much more than salvation from hell to heaven; it requires the way of the cross."

As Mary read the letter and reflected again on the biblical view of human history, she realized that there was something beyond both optimism that ignores pain in the world and pessimism that says that's all there is. "I came to understand that biblical hope in Jesus makes me an incredible realist," she says. "I can go into the world of pain and sit with people in their pain and suffering. I can try to understand the illusions that they grasp hold of and lovingly challenge them. I have learned to hope, not despite the suffering, but in the midst of it."

Mary was living in the United States in June 1989, when government tanks rolled into Tienanmen Square and crushed the budding democracy movement, and she wept as she watched that tragedy unfolding. "I understood as never before that hope allows my heart to break at the evil, illusion and suffering we live among in this world."

Later she had the chance to talk with some Chinese intellectuals about the meaning of hope. They had seen some of their own students killed in Tienanmen Square, yet they wondered how they would respond when their turn came to exercise political leadership and power in China. They asked themselves what would keep them from becoming corrupt and oppressive. And one person turned to Mary with the question "If I stay outside the community of hope you speak of, if I don't believe in your Jesus, do I have any other hope to offer the world?"

Mary's willingness to identify with China's students and intellectuals, to understand their dreams and fears, to suffer with them and stand beside them, had given her an opportunity to demonstrate the powerful hope of the gospel. The people of God are people defined by hope: hope of eternal life, hope of God's comfort in our own lives and struggles. Yet our hope is not limited to ourselves. It is a radical hope that challenges all the despair and all the false hopes of a world caught in the trauma of sin and evil.

It was this hope the apostle Paul pointed to when he spoke of "Christ in you, the hope of glory" (Col 1:27). That hope, which energized the first Christians to take the good news to the furthest reaches of the known world, works powerfully in God's people today. The signposts of hope are evident all around us. Some are broadcast on the evening news. We see joyful Berliners dismantling the Wall. And we rejoice in South Korea's gigantic churches and blossoming mission movement. Other signs of hope are known by only a few—in the quiet witness of a faithful teacher bringing love and hope to one inner-city child at a time, or in the still, small voice of the Lord assuring a hurting child of his love.

The stories that follow celebrate hope in Christ and call us anew to the task of bringing hope to men and women of every nation, tongue and tribe.

Questions for Groups or Individuals

1. Share the story of how you first encountered hope in Jesus Christ with others in your group or with one other person this week.

2. What evidence of hope in the world do you see today? (Think of recent news events or people you know who demonstrate hope through their lives.)

3. The chapter outlines the response Mary's professor gave to answer her in her crisis of faith. In your own words, summarize the biblical understanding of humanity's plight and God's solution.

For Further Study

Urbana Tapes

Plenary Session Video #1, *God So Loved the World,* Mary Fisher.

Audio #7188, "Jesus Christ: Hope of the World," Mary Fisher.

2

Lord of
the Universe

When the British invaded the Falkland Islands in 1982, Luis Bush found himself in a crisis. He was an Argentine citizen, born of an Argentine father and a British mother. At the time he was serving as a missionary in El Salvador, and the Salvadorans were rooting for Argentina. They asked him, "Who do you think those islands belong to?" Luis thought about it and answered, "I think those islands belong to the Lord Jesus Christ. He is the Lord of the universe and the Lord of those islands."

The personal dilemma Luis experienced was magnified immensely for young people in Argentina. The war and the upheaval that followed it led to a crisis of authority. "But in the midst of the chaos," Luis says, "the written Word and the living

Word of God were lifted up and thousands of Argentinians came to recognize that it is Jesus who is Lord."

God's Calling

Luis tells of one of the unlikely ministers whom God raised up to fill the leadership vacuum in Argentina. "Carlos Anacondia was a businessman and deacon. One Wednesday evening the pastor of the small church he was attending did not show up, and he was invited to give a short message. Despite the encouragement of his wife who was sitting beside him, he did not budge. A second time his name was mentioned, but he said to himself, 'I can't preach.' Even with his wife's nudging he did not move. The third time his wife's nudge became a jab, and he jumped up and spoke on the lordship and authority of Christ.

"God blessed his Word, and so he was invited to speak again. At first he preached in the church, but it was too small, so he would go to the soccer fields, set up his equipment and preach. Hundreds, then thousands came to his meetings. In the meetings held in one city, Mar del Plata, 90,000 public decisions were made for Christ. Never had anything like this been seen in Argentina."

The lordship of Christ is a powerful message of hope for a world that has seen many of its symbols of power and authority unmasked and discredited. The apostle Paul, writing to Colossian Christians in the first century, emphasized the authority of Christ, as the fullness of God's person and the hope of the fulfillment of God's plan.

He begins his letter with thanksgiving for what God is doing in their midst and prayer for them. He describes them as people of hope—living out "because of the hope laid up for you in heaven" (Col 1:5). Then puts their hope in the context of the larger work of God in the world: "All over the world this gospel is bearing fruit and growing" (Col 1:6). Indeed, within three decades of Pentecost, there were Christians in almost every corner of the Roman Empire. Paul was reminding the Colossians that the Lord they had put their faith in was Lord of all the world, that their hope was a big enough hope for all the peoples of the earth. The same is true today.

The Spread of the Gospel

At the beginning of this century more than 90 per cent of Christians lived in the West. Today nearly 80 per cent of the church lives outside the West. All over our world—from the universities of China to the villages of India to the townships of South Africa to the barrios of São Paulo to the skyscrapers of London and New York—the gospel is growing and bearing fruit. Our hope is strengthened by the faithful witness of God's people all around the globe who are living out their faith in God and love for one another.

But ultimately our hope is rooted in the person of Jesus Christ. In the first chapter of Colossians, Paul provides what has been called a "full-length portrait of Christ." Christ's participation in creation demonstrates his right to rule over all creation—"whether thrones or powers or rulers or authorities" (Col 1:16). And he is Lord of the church, as its redeemer and the reconciler of the universe.

Hope in the Midst of Hopelessness

Luis Bush describes how the supremacy and sufficiency of Christ brought real hope in a desperate situation, in the midst of civil war in El Salvador, where he lived for seven years. "It was a hopeless situation economically because there was 40 per cent unemployment. Politically, it was hopelessly unstable; 50,000 people lost their lives, mainly young people. Yet it was the time I've experienced some of the greatest hope among the Lord's people in the need to come to the Lord and find in him our source of hope. At other times we hope in our circumstances, our comfort zones, or money in the bank, but there all of us had to cast ourselves on the Lord." People who had put their trust in Jesus and found him faithful had a tremendous impact on those around them too. Between 1974 and 1984, the number of evangelical Christians in El Salvador tripled.

Jesus is Lord over everything. He is also the hope for the fulfillment of God's purposes in world. Paul states boldly: "This is the gospel that you have heard and that has been proclaimed to every creature under heaven" (Col 1:25). Paul's concern was for fulfillment, for completion of God's work of redemption. It's our concern, too, as we look at a world that groans under the burden of sin.

As the world's population passes six billion some time this decade, more than four billion people will still be outside of Christ's lordship. Of these, one expert estimates that about 1.3 billion are members of the 2,000 ethnolinguistic people groups that have no access to the good news within their culture.[1]

It was the task of proclaiming the gospel to every creature that motivated Paul and allowed him to say, "I rejoice in what was suffered for you, and I fill up in my flesh what is still lacking in regard to Christ's afflictions" (Col 1:24). Paul's lifestyle was one of sacrifice and servanthood. Those remain the earmarks of Christians committed to fulfillment of God's will for the world, who lay aside the comforts of their own cultures, enter into the suffering of the poor, and listen to the brokenhearted.

The Mystery of God's Plan

Paul focuses his discussion of the fulfillment of God's plan on the idea of "mystery." What Paul means by the word *mystery* is not a puzzle to be solved—a kind of cosmic whodunit—but rather something that was hidden and now has been revealed. J. B. Phillips paraphrases Colossians 1:26-27 in this way: "That sacred mystery which up till now has been hidden in every age and every generation, but which is now as clear as daylight to those who love God. They are those to whom God has planned to give a vision of the full wonder and splendor of his secret plan for the nations. And the secret is simply this: Christ in you! Yes, Christ in you bringing with him the hope of all the glorious things to come."

The mystery of God's plan for the world is that all the fullness of God which was seen in Jesus is now in us as believers. In other words, God intends to work through his people to make himself known among the nations and to complete the work of reconciliation. Paul describes it this way: "And he has committed to us the message of reconciliation. We are therefore Christ's ambassadors, as though God were making his appeal through us" (2 Cor 5:19-20).

Called into Partnership

The call of God to partnership with him in his work of reconciling the world to himself resonates deeply in the heart of those who love the Lord. Paul Leary describes his response to the challenge of mission as he heard it as a student at Urbana 79. "This call from God was not packaged in slick slogans promising me the good life, but more than anything I had ever heard, the idea of giving my life as a witness gave me a sense of purpose."

As stirring as the call to go into the world as a witness can be, there is another reality that Christians face as they contemplate a life of service—their own sense of inadequacy. "Christ in you, the hope of glory" can sound like empty words to someone dealing with the hurt of a broken home or struggling with the devastation of a loved one's addiction. For all of us, the experience of hope on a personal level of Christ meeting us and healing us in the places of deepest need and pain in our lives becomes a building block for a broader hope. When Christ has made a difference in our lives, we can more easily believe that he will work through us to make a difference in the world.

Questions for Groups or Individuals

1. Luis Bush described the impact of Christ's lordship in the midst of the hardships of El Salvador's civil war. How does Christ's lordship make a difference in the way you think or feel about difficult situations in your life?

2. Read Colossians 1. List the specific descriptions of Christ in verses 13-20.

What do each of these attributes mean to you personally?

3. What is the mystery of God's plan (Col 1:25-27)?

4. How would you describe God's purpose in human history? (You might want to look at Gen 12:1-3; Mt 24:14 and 28:18-20; Gal 3:6-9; Rev 7:9.)

5. What is your part in God's plan, as you understand it today?

6. What one thing can you do today as one of Christ's ambassadors?

For Further Study

Urbana Tapes

Plenary Session Video #2, *Colossians 1: Lordship of Christ,* Luis
   Bush.

Audio #7186, "Colossians 1: Lordship of Christ," Luis Bush.

Bible Studies

Reapsome, Martha. *Colossians & Philemon: Finding Fulfillment in Christ.* A Lifeguide® Bible Study. Downers Grove, Ill.: InterVarsity Press, 1989.

3

Hope for Broken People

I n 1971, my wife, Shelby, and I were serving with Wycliffe
Bible Translators in Papua New Guinea. We had just
started our second term after a very busy and stressful
year of furlough, and we were feeling like we hadn't experienced the refreshment and renewal we needed to get through
the next three or four years on the field.

While we were gone, some of our best friends on the field
were introduced to prayer for the healing of memories, and
when they told us about it, we were interested. They explained
that they weren't praying for God to take away our memories—
no one wants that—but that he would heal the pain of those
memories.

We had both grown up in dysfunctional families. My missionary parents were so dedicated to their ministry that I never felt sure of my father's love, and Shelby's dad had walked out on the family when she was thirteen. I had been reconciled to my father, but there was still a reservoir of anger and insecurity in me that influenced my behavior.

I had a habit of being extremely critical, especially of Shelby. I picked on her for everything. She didn't dress right. She didn't feed the children right. She didn't do anything right. But she wasn't the only one I criticized. I remember sitting in the back row of our missionary fellowship on Sunday mornings, mentally criticizing each of my colleagues as I looked at the back of their heads.

Sam and Nancy prayed for us, asking God to heal the hurt of past memories. I didn't feel any different after they prayed, but as days and weeks passed I noticed dramatic changes in my life. I stopped criticizing Shelby. The following Sunday, I sat in my usual spot in the back of church and found myself thinking warm thoughts about my friends, praying prayers of blessing over them.

Getting Past the Anger

God had healed a wound in my heart that had been the source of destructive attitudes. That was just one step in the journey I've been on since giving my life to Christ when I was nineteen. At first I thought that God would just take away the anger and hurts of my turbulent, rebellious youth, but I found it wasn't that simple.

My relationship with my father was punctuated with conflict, from the time I was twelve and decided to join my older brother, Frank, in our two-holer outhouse for a smoke. My father caught me on my way back into the house.

"You've been smoking!" he said.

I answered with a rude remark.

"You go into your bedroom and take down your Levis," he ordered.

"I'll go into the bedroom, but I won't take down my Levis," I answered.

A few minutes later he came in, pulling off his two-inch leather belt. He kept saying, "You promise me you'll never smoke again"

I answered, "I promise you I'll learn to smoke."

Finally, he gave up in exhaustion. I hitched a ride into town, bought a pack of Pall Mall's, found a friend who smoked and asked him to teach me.

Truancy was a way of life for me during my high-school years. I quit a number of times. Once, when I was about fourteen, I went on a trip to Florida to visit Frank. While I was with him I got a letter from my dad. I tore the envelope open in my excitement. Most of the letter reminded me of my debts to Dad, including the bus fare for my trip. He asked me how I intended to pay it back. But he signed the letter, "Love, Dad."

Love, Dad! My dad loved me! I had never heard him say those words. I was convinced he didn't love me. But he said so there, in writing. I carried that letter around in my wallet until it wore out, and I could no longer read "Love, Dad."

After I became a Christian, there was a lot of healing that needed to take place in my relationship with my father. I lived with my parents for three years while I was in college, and I learned to respect them and see things from their perspective even when I didn't agree with them. But there still came a day when I felt a deep conviction to ask my father for his forgiveness. I went to him and said, "Dad, will you forgive me for being such a rebellious son? Would you forgive me for my harsh, angry words?" And he granted me that forgiveness. My recovery has come in fits and starts, sometimes I've been aware of God's healing touch, sometimes it has seemed like I've made the same mistake a hundred times and have to keep relearning the lesson. Through it all, he has allowed me the privilege of serving in mission work—teaching missionary kids in Papua New Guinea, serving Wycliffe's international offices, helping to send English teachers to China, and now mobilizing students to go all over the world through Urbana. The struggles and weaknesses are still with me, but I have discovered that his strength is made perfect in my weakness.

Dan Everett is a linguist and translator working on giving the Piraha people in Brazil the New Testament in their own language. Dan comes from a broken family. Dan's mother died when he was eleven. Three years later, his biological father took him to live at his house near the Mexican border. It was his introduction to a destructive lifestyle that has affected him for many years.

"One night my dad took me to Mexico and we stayed out all night long, my first time to get drunk and meet prostitutes. It wasn't my last. Soon, I learned that you could buy marijuana, 'speed,' and about anything else in Mexico. I started making regular trips down to buy and bring back drugs." Dan started a rock band and had one clear purpose in life: "To get famous or die before I was 25."

That's where Dan was when he met Steve Graham, a fellow high schooler who had lived with his missionary parents in Brazil. Steve invited Dan home to meet his family, and Dan was impressed with them. Dan says, "This family had a love, faith and quality of home life that I had never seen before. I asked

God to give me what these people had."

Through the witness of the entire family, especially Steve's father, Al, Dan became a Christian. "I immediately stopped using drugs," he recalls. "Just had no use for them anymore. Over the next months I took many of my friends to meet Al. They would spend time talking to Al in his room and come out with a smile on their face and a New Testament in their hands."

A few years later Dan married Keren Graham, and together they committed themselves to the task of bringing the Bible's message of hope to people who have never heard it. "Through my brokenness, God made me stronger and more effective than I could have ever imagined," says Dan. But success hasn't come without struggles with the residues of that past brokenness, particularly anger and cynicism.

"At one point in my life after I had been married for about two or three years, I thought that those things were completely gone." He found them resurfacing on the mission field in times of stress, when they were living in the Brazilian jungle with the Piraha tribe and someone in the family became ill. "They would still come to me, business as usual, asking for things or asking for help. I realized that my reaction to them was not only negative but much more negative then I could explain. And I realized that there was still anger and bitterness in me that I had to deal with."

Living in a Dysfunctional Family

There is hardly a young person in North America who doesn't have to deal with the effects of a dysfunctional home. More than a million families are fragmented by divorce each year. Half the marriages made today will end in divorce, demographers predict. A third of the children born in the 1980s will live in a stepfamily before they are eighteen. An estimated twelve million people in the United States are alcoholics, and another 22 million adult children of alcoholics struggle with the scars left by their childhood experiences. By the age of sixteen, one out of four girls has been sexually abused. Physical violence characterizes some fifteen million American families. The stress of poverty compounds these other problems. Today one out of four children is being raised by a single parent and one out of five children lives in poverty. Unfortunately, these statistics apply to the dedicated Christian young people who came to Urbana 90.

Dysfunctional families are ones in which rigid rules dictate behavior and communication is limited. Feelings are not freely expressed in these homes, but rather suppressed or denied. Sometimes they only emerge years later as inexplicable anger or insecurity. People who grow up in dysfunctional families often have problems with self-esteem, for which they compensate either with utter rebellion or superachievement.

The Healing Process

Restoration and recovery from a dysfunctional background can take many forms, yet several themes are evident in the stories of those who testify to God's healing in their lives. For some the most important step is acknowledging the painful reality of the past and starting to deal with it. Jan Frank, who has written about her experience as a victim of sexual abuse in *Out of the Shadows,* says, "A pivotal scripture for me was Psalm 51:6 that says, 'Surely you desire truth in the inner parts; you teach me wisdom in the inmost place.' As I began to pray that, the Lord really spoke to me and said, 'The wounds of the past have not been healed. We need to bring those out into the light. We need to expose them so that I can heal you totally from the inside out,' whereas I had tried all those years to heal myself from the outside in."

For many people from dysfunctional backgrounds, bringing the hurts into the light means learning to deal with emotions that may have been repressed for a long time. For Christians, it may mean learning to forgive a family member who has caused deep hurt.

Mary Anne Voelkel, who serves with Latin American Mission in Colombia, discovered this in relation to her alcoholic father. "The place of healing in my life began when I recognized I was angry. I was complaining to God in my devotions one day: 'How come my father's like this? Why doesn't he change?' And the Lord spoke to me out of Matthew 18. He reminded me that he had forgiven me ten million talents of sinfulness in my own life. I recognized that the Lord said, 'Mary Anne, I've forgiven you everything. Can you not forgive your father who hasn't a penny inside to pay you back?' And I was humbled and went down on my knees and asked the Lord to forgive me."

Forgiveness doesn't mean pretending that the painful events of the past didn't happen. People who grew up in dysfunctional homes experienced parents who let them down or abused them. Forgiveness breaks the power of those hurts, though. Without forgiveness, anger turns into bitterness, which takes root in our lives and wreaks all kinds of destruction.

God Wants to Heal You

The ultimate key for wounded people is the assurance that God wants to heal them, and the pages of Scripture abound with God's concern for broken hearts and hurting people. Just look at the Scripture Jesus read to inaugurate his public ministry:

The Spirit of the Sovereign LORD is on me,
  because the LORD has anointed me
  to preach good news to the poor.
He has sent me to bind up the brokenhearted,
  to proclaim freedom for the captives
  and release from darkness for the prisoners,
to proclaim the year of the LORD's favor
  and the day of vengeance of our God,
to comfort all who mourn,
  and provide for those who grieve in Zion—
to bestow on them a crown of beauty
  instead of ashes,
the oil of gladness
  instead of mourning,
and a garment of praise
  instead of a spirit of despair.
They will be called oaks of righteousness,
  a planting of the LORD
  for the display of his splendor. (Is 61:1-3)

The work of Christ in his people is the process of transforming brokenhearted captives cowering in the dark into "oaks of righteousness" who demonstrate to others what grace is all about.

Isaac Canales grew up in a Christian home. His father was a pastor of inner-city churches in Los Angeles. As a boy, he would join his father in selling homemade tamales out of the back of the family station wagon throughout Watts and surrounding areas, earning money to pay for their church building. As a teen, though, he rebelled.

"I was doing a lot of drugs and playing the trumpet in bars and dance halls," Isaac recalls. "Then on an LSD trip in 1971,

I had a very powerful, life-changing experience, where I actually felt I was coming face to face with the ugliness in myself, and I didn't know how to handle it. The only thing I could think about was killing myself, because it was just so ugly—knowing that I was a liar, a hypocrite, full of sin. I went and talked to my Dad—it was about three in the morning—and he assured me that I didn't have to kill myself because Christ has already died in my place. It made a whole lot of sense. And I was just so exhilarated that Christ had taken my place, and I didn't have to end it with a .45 automatic."

The good news of the Gospel is that we aren't alone in that confrontation with our pain and sin. We have hope because of Jesus. In the words of Glandion Carney, "I think the Good News is the hope that Jesus Christ gives us when we literally throw ourselves on him, and he then picks up the pieces and puts us back together again. There's nothing wrong with being broken. It's just a matter of how you get up again, and how the pieces come back together again."

Ministering to Others

One of the important ways that the pieces come back together is when people in the process of being healed take the risk of sharing their story with another hurting person and pointing them to the Healer. That's what Jan Frank discovered as she told her story to other victims of abuse: "Every time I shared it was as though God was saying 'I'm going to put the salve over your wound as you're sharing with another person.' "

Our brokenness can be a bridge to ministry and an important way of lending credibility to the truth we share. "If I'm sharing Christ, it is never done void of the autobiographical," says Elward Ellis, president of Destiny, an organization committed to mobilizing African-American Christians for mission. "We are really impressed by our struggles, whatever the issues in our lives, we are impressed by the force and the strength of them. We wonder sometimes, 'Is God able to deal with this?' I think that transparency is important. I don't mean messy, irresponsible and reckless sharing of stuff, but an illustration of how God met me, even when it risks a public image. Or maybe God hasn't yet met me in my struggle. I like Paul [in Philippians]. He is honest. He's preaching what we ought to be like, but then he feels it necessary to say 'I haven't got there yet.' "

Elward came from a family where his father took off when he was seven. "My mother had to raise us by herself in a family that was looking down on us because she had a baby out of wedlock. We were poor—I mean, we didn't have anything to eat—but to certain people you could let that be known, and with other people you had to act like you'd had a full meal. You had to learn how to lie about hunger."

He points to a tendency among evangelicals to emphasize their doctrinal understanding of God and salvation, but neglect the biblical teachings on human nature. "My church gave me a very high sense of what I was, and that was something to aspire to, that in Christ I'm a new creature. But what about my tendency to lie rather than be embarrassed? What about my tendency sometimes to manipulate people's emotions? What about the things I know about myself that are wrong and malicious and intentional?"

Without an understanding that we are indeed new creatures in Christ and yet at the same time, we still need to be renewed and transformed in the daily realities of our lives, it's easy to think that weakness is something to be hidden or denied. Too often Christians, especially those in public ministry, invest a lot of time and energy in projecting an image they want others to have of them—which works against their own growth as well as cutting them off from accountability to others. "For every minute of whatever we want people to see that we succeed in pulling off," says Elward, "we probably have an hour's worth of retardation going on."

Accepting the reality of our fallen nature can actually be a source of hope, when we see it in light of God's promise to transform us from the inside out. "Now we are children of God, and what we will be has not yet been made known. But we know that when he appears, we shall be like him, for we shall see him as he is" (1 Jn 3:2).

"I don't take what I am and where I am today as the end of the story," says Elward. "That's my hope, and that's what I share with students, because if I had to stop where I am and look in the mirror that would be overwhelming. If there was no growth beyond that, then I would be despairing. But I can accept myself, I can cope with me, because I have hope that every day, like a clock on the wall, the Spirit of God is working in me. I'm going to be somewhere else five years from now, though when you look at me today, you won't see the hands move."

As painful as confronting our brokenness can be, in the light of Christ's love and commitment to make us whole and holy persons, it can be an experience of great hope and freedom. And the hope we encounter when we give up trying to make ourselves "okay" is what propels us into the world to spread the news of our loving Savior.

Questions for Groups or Individuals

1. What kinds of brokenness are you aware of in the expe-

riences of people around you—perhaps in your own family or in members of your church or fellowship or circle of friends?

2. Describe the consequences of that brokenness in terms of behavior and attitudes.

3. Review the stories and quotes in the chapter. Which ones challenge you or give you hope? Why?

4. How would you encourage a friend who was experiencing brokenness? (What scriptural truths would you point to? What experiences would you share?)

For Further Study
Urbana Tapes
Plenary Session Video #2, *Strongest in the Broken Places: Hope for the Hurting,* Dan Harrison.
Audio #7188, "Strongest in the Broken Places: Hope for the Hurting," Dan Harrison.
Picking Up the Pieces, 2100 Productions Video.

Bible Studies
Harrison, Dan. *Healing for Broken People.* Global Issues Bible Studies. Downers Grove, Ill.: InterVarsity Press, 1990.

Books
Harrison, Dan. *Strongest in the Broken Places.* Downers Grove, Ill.: InterVarsity Press, 1990.
The Twelve Steps—A Spiritual Journey. San Diego: Recovery Publications, 1988.

4

Jesus:
Our Only Hope

Steve Hayner tells the story of a conversation he once had with a fellow airline passenger, a young woman who introduced herself during the flight as a "white witch."

"I believe in using my magical powers only for good," she explained.

"And how do you know what is good?" Steve asked.

Perhaps at no other time in human history have so many conflicting versions of what is true and what is good competed for people's attention. Islam's claim of universal brotherhood attracts minorities in North American cities, even as its influence is growing around the world. Eastern religious concepts such as reincarnation have gained credibility in the West under the guise of the New Age Movement's brand of spiritual awareness. Secular, materialist culture is being confronted through mediums and seances. In the marketplace of these competing systems, Jesus' claim about himself is as radical today as it was 2000 years ago: "I am the way and the truth and the life. No one comes to the Father except through me" (Jn 14:6).

Is Christ the Answer?

Missiologists estimate that well over a billion people remain isolated geographically or culturally from a meaningful witness to Jesus Christ. Development experts tell us one billion people live in absolute poverty, unable to meet their basic needs for food, shelter, water and health care. War and famine force tens of millions to live as refugees. Unchecked urbanization brings millions of people into overburdened cities each year, where most of them live as squatters in dire poverty. Economies in the Two-Thirds World stagger under the weight of debt owed to developed countries and the urge to compete in the worldwide arms race.

Can we be sure that Jesus is the only true hope as we confront this aching world?

"The best way to show that false teaching is false is to show how glorious Jesus is," says Ajith Fernando, national director of Youth For Christ in Sri Lanka. In his letter to the Colossians, the apostle Paul confronts the false teachers of his day by pointing out how shallow their claims are when confronted by the glories of Christ.

Paul explains that his purpose is to encourage the believers, "so that they may have the full riches of complete understanding, in order that they may know the mystery of God, namely, Christ" (Col 2:2). These brief phrases are packed with superlatives—"full riches," "complete understanding," even the Greek word translated "know" is an emphatic word, *epignosis*. It stands in contrast to the teachings of the gnostics, who claimed that their brand of special knowledge (or *gnosis*) gave access to God. Other religious teachers claim to teach truth, Paul is saying, but the message he has been entrusted with is the Truth. The Bible isn't simply the record of some peoples' religious experiences. It is God's revelation of himself to humankind. And according to Scripture, the mystery of God isn't some secret knowledge. It isn't a complex philosophical system. The mystery of God, God's ultimate revelation of truth, is a person: Jesus Christ.

Stanley Jones, an American missionary to India in the early part of this century, sought to communicate the uniqueness of Christ to Hindu people. One day he was giving a lecture to a Hindu audience, where he was introduced by the governor of the state, who stated, "I shall reserve my remarks for the close of the address. For no matter what the speaker says, I will find parallel things in our own sacred books." But at the end of the lecture, the governor had nothing to say. Stanley Jones had not presented "things" or "truths" or "principles." He had presented Jesus Christ.

And that person is like no other human being who ever lived. "For in Christ all the fullness of the Deity lives in bodily form" (Col 2:9). Paul argues against the "hollow and deceptive philosophies" of the false teachers of his day, with their stringent rules of behavior and special observances. These things are not necessary, Paul claims, because all the fullness of God has been revealed in Christ. He is all we need to know in order to know God fully. God is not far away from us, remote and unknowable. He has put on human flesh and become a brother to us. And through the incarnation, "we have seen his glory, . . . full of grace and truth" (Jn 1:14).

Meeting Jesus Personally

Abdul wanted to know God from the time he was very young. Born into a Muslim family in Iran, he felt the teaching of the prophet Mohammed didn't fulfill this longing. "I felt that the laws, though good, were empty, leaving me with no relationship with God, whoever he was." Sent to the United States to study as a 15-year-old, he quickly discovered his understanding of immigration law was inadequate too. He was deported.

Abdul found himself on a bizarre odyssey as he was put on a plane back to Iran just as the revolution began. Tehran's international airport was closed. The plane landed in Turkey, and Abdul realized his passport was still in New York. He was jailed as an illegal immigrant.

While Abdul was in jail, he met a Pakistani Christian who offered him comfort. Later, he found himself in India. "I became very ill and while in the hospital, I experienced an overwhelming sense of peace, that Someone was with me." By the time he finally made it to Oregon, Abdul was very eager to find out who had been taking care of him.

"God brought some Christian friends into my life and through their diligent persuasion all the pieces of my life came together and I realized who was taking care of me during those four months I was lost in the world." The personal reality of Jesus Christ changed Abdul's life, despite the barriers of culture and religion.

The gospel's ability to speak to people of all cultures, indeed its claim on all peoples, comes from Jesus' lordship over all the world, seen in the way Paul describes him in Colossians 1—2. All things were created by him. He is before all things. In him all things hold together. In everything he might have supremacy. God was pleased to have all his fullness dwell in him and to reconcile to himself all things. In Christ are all the treasures of wisdom and knowledge. He forgave all our sins. The picture Paul paints is of an absolute Lord.

Jesus is Lord of all. And the corollary to the word *all* is only. If he is indeed Lord of all, then he is the only Lord.

Ajith Fernando recalls an incident that brought home the reality of Christ's lordship in a new way. He was applying for a visa to go to England and had run into some problems in getting it. So he sat down to write a letter to the British ambassador. "This man is a big fellow, so I thought I must address him as 'Your Excellency.' After all, he is the ambassador of the Queen of England. Then the thought came to me that I am an ambassador of the King of the Queen of England."

The Power of the Resurrection

This conviction that he was an ambassador of the King of all kings sent Paul and his band of evangelists to every center and city of the Roman Empire they could get to. Standing among a somewhat hostile crowd of Greek philosophers and religious speculators in Athens, Paul preached a very contextualized sermon. He didn't even mention Jesus' name, but spoke of "the man [God] has appointed." The core of his message was that "God commands all people everywhere to repent." Christ's lordship demands a response from every human being. And the most compelling evidence Paul offered for this remarkable claim was: "He has given proof of this to all men by raising him from the dead" (Acts 17:31).

For the early church the resurrection was the central event of its history. As the eleven apostles chose a replacement for Judas, their chief concern was to elect someone who could be a witness to the resurrection. The resurrection figured prominently in their preaching. When Paul summed up the gospel in 1 Corinthians 15, he ended with a long list of people who had seen the risen Christ, many of whom were still alive at the time he wrote the letter.

Our hope is based on the historical fact that Jesus was raised from the dead. If that's not true, Paul said to the Corinthians, "your faith is futile; you are still in your sins" (1 Cor 15:17). The Christian gospel is unique because it does for us what all of human religion claims but fails to provide: a new life, a solution to the problem of sin. "When you were dead in your sins and in the uncircumcision of your sinful nature, God made you alive with Christ" (Col 2:13). The new life Christ gives us is our only hope for dealing with sin, whether in our own life or in the sinful systems of the world. Human methods of attaining righteousness, Paul says, "have an appearance of wisdom, . . . but they lack any value in restraining sensual indulgence" (Col 2:23).

Source of Hope

This certainty of the power of the resurrection gives hope even in the most difficult circumstances, a hope I saw demonstrated in the story of my parents' ministry among Tibetans in Western China. They began their ministry in a village called Hetsuohen in 1923, and after two years saw the first convert, a young chieftain named Wan De Ker, who became a bold witness to Christ. He attracted so much interest, in fact, that two weeks after his conversion the local Buddhist authorities killed him, stuffed his mouth with stones and dragged his body behind a horse through the center of the town. The mission leaders advised my parents to move, but they felt sure of their call to that place. They stayed there another twenty years, serving the people in a variety of ways and nurturing a handful of secret believers. Some might have wondered whether my parents' sacrifice was worth it, judging from the limited results they saw. However, they never doubted that their responsibility was to be faithful to God's call and to put their hope in his power to change lives.

I remember the day in the early 1960s when my parents received a letter from a Swedish missionary working with Tibetan refugees in India. This missionary had gone to some lengths to track down the faithful couple the Tibetans described as those who had set broken bones, cured venereal disease and always told the Jesus story. He included a long list of those who had become Christians, and he wanted my parents to know that the harvest they had helped to sow was being reaped. Their hope was not in vain. The story of God's work among the Tibetan people they had loved and served hadn't ended with Wan De Ker's death or with the end of Western missions in China.

People who have been made alive in Christ are people of hope. The catastrophic results of the Fall are apparent everywhere around us—in broken families, abused children, in urban crime and poverty, in unjust economic systems and religions that keep millions in bondage, in war and violence, and in racism and oppression.

But this is not the end of the story.

Jesus is God's revelation to a sinful world. As he walked among the poor and ate with sinners, all the fullness of the Deity was being expressed in human form. "And you have been given fullness in Christ." As people reborn into that same fullness we have a responsibility to a dying world. It is the unique gift of Christ that is both our motivation and the hope we have to offer.

Questions for Groups or Individuals

1. Read Colossians 2. What are some of the "hollow and deceptive philosophies" you encounter on campus or in the workplace?

2. What does the Bible claim to be (see 2 Tim 3:16; Lk 1:1-3; 1 Jn 1:3)?

Have you found it to be that?

3. Look at Paul's sermon to the Athenians in Acts 17:16-34. How does Paul make the claim that Jesus' Lordship and salvation applies to Greeks as well as to Jews?

How might you use such an approach in sharing with a non-Christian you know?

4. How does the resurrection of Jesus give you hope?

5. Discuss Adbul's story of meeting Christ. How did the gospel cross cultural barriers in his life?

For Further Study

Urbana Tapes

Plenary Session Video #4, Ajith Fernando.

Audio #7186, "Colossians 2: The Uniqueness of Christ," Ajith Fernando.

Books

Bruce, F. F. *The New Testament Documents: Are They Reliable?* 5th ed. Downers Grove, Ill.: InterVarsity Press, 1960.

Fernando, Ajith. *The Christian's Attitude Toward World Religions.* Wheaton, Ill.: Tyndale, 1987.

McDowell, Josh. *Evidence that Demands a Verdict,* rev. ed. San Bernardino, Calif.: Here's Life, 1979.

5

The Creative
Access World

ake a look at map 1. The box (or window) drawn, following
lines 10 degrees and 40 degrees north of the equator, from
the western edge of Africa to the Pacific Ocean, defines
the biggest challenge facing the church today. This "10/40 window" defines the part of our world "where the evidence of
Christ's lordship is strangely missing," in the words of Luis
Bush, president of Partners International. The region stretches
from the countries of North Africa, through the Middle East,
across much of the southern Soviet Union with its large Muslim population, through Pakistan, India and Burma, into
Southeast Asia and Japan.

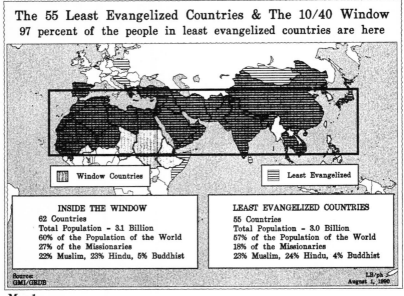

The 55 Least Evangelized Countries & The 10/40 Window
97 percent of the people in least evangelized countries are here

Window Countries   Least Evangelized

INSIDE THE WINDOW
62 Countries
Total Population - 3.1 Billion
60% of the Population of the World
27% of the Missionaries
22% Muslim, 23% Hindu, 5% Buddhist

LEAST EVANGELIZED COUNTRIES
55 Countries
Total Population - 3.0 Billion
57% of the Population of the World
18% of the Missionaries
23% Muslim, 24% Hindu, 4% Buddhist

Source:
GMI/GRDB
LB/ph
August 1, 1990

Map 1

Within this huge region lie 55 of the world's least evangelized countries. According to David Barrett, perhaps the world's foremost expert on the growth of Christianity around the world, more than 90 per cent of the world's unreached people groups—those without a substantial witness within their own culture—live within this window.

Most of these countries are what we call the "creative access" countries. Christians cannot normally enter these nations with a missionary visa. However, they do find roles as "tentmakers," a term derived from the way the apostle Paul supported himself during some of his missionary journeys by making tents. Modern-day tentmakers enter countries as students or teachers, or serve the needs of the host country through professional skills or business opportunities. Legal restrictions on churches and "proselytizing" may dictate other "creative" ways of sharing the good news and building fellowships of believers.

The 10/40 window represents great physical as well as spiritual poverty. As map 2 illustrates, more than 80 per cent of the world's poorest people live within this region.

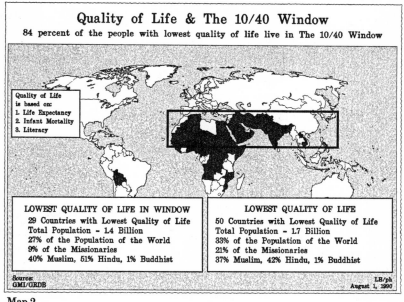

Map 2

Malnutrition and lack of basic health care threaten the very existence of close to a billion people. Without access to clean water, many children die of simple, preventable diseases like diarrhea, and others face crippling disabilities. In many of these cultures, women do as much physical labor as men, but eat last and least, even when pregnant or nursing. Illiteracy keeps millions of adults in the bondage of ignorance and injustice. In 1987 alone, 14 million people were refugees uprooted from their home country by war or famine.[1] Millions more were internally displaced. The toll of humankind's sin and Satan's demonic control of societies and structures in this region is staggering.

Meeting the Challenge

A closer look at this 10/40 window, according to George Otis, Jr., reveals two important factors: the task is getting smaller, but it is becoming more difficult.

The first observation is based on looking at what is not contained within the strategic window. In North and South America, Europe and Australia the gospel has made a substantial impact. Africa below the Sahara is the first continent in history to go from being majority non-Christian to majority Christian in a single century. Additionally, the dramatic changes that have occurred in Eastern Europe reveal a widespread spiritual hunger and responsiveness. And the face of Latin America is being transformed by the explosion of evangelical and Pentecostal churches there. Finally as much as 30 per cent of Guatemala's population is Protestant, including Jorge Serrano Elias, elected president in January 1991.

At the same time other factors are causing the task to become more difficult. With the decline and debunking of Marxism as a major world force, other ideological and spiritual forces, chief among them Islam, have grown in influence. The ability of militant Islam to capture the world stage through military power and terrorist zeal has led James Bill of the University of Texas to declare that "over the next 40 years populist Islam will be the most important ideological force in the world."[2]

At the geographical center of the 10/40 window lies the region known as the cradle of civilization. This was the stage upon which much of the biblical drama was played out. And today, occupying this cradle region are Iran and Iraq, two countries which over the past dozen years have been focal points for the confrontation between Islam and the rest of the world. Despite the daunting challenge ahead, the evidence abounds that the 10/40 window is actually shrinking. Significant inroads are being made along its periphery, even in some of the most restricted and underevangelized places on earth.

Mongolia, for many years considered the most unreached nation on earth, has begun to crack its doors open to the gospel. On two occasions in late 1990, more than 1,000 pounds of Christian literature brought into the country have been snapped up in a matter of minutes. The government recently invited both the Peace Corps and a Christian organization to bring in English teachers, opening up opportunities for Western Christians to live in a country that has been one of the most isolated since it became a Soviet satellite in 1924. Even Albania, the only nation which ever declared religion completely illegal, has repealed its Stalinist laws and has begun to open its borders.

Signs of Hope
But perhaps more significant than the inroads being made on the edges of the 10/40 window, are signs of hope that a new day may be dawning for the heart of this region.

The New Testament has a word for times of great opportunity: *kairos. Kairos* means "time," not time measured by a clock, with each minute having the same value as the one before it and the one after it. *Kairos* refers to a special time, the fullness of time, the right time for something to happen. The dramatic events that have transformed the face of Eastern Europe and the Soviet Union point to a *kairos* moment of opportunity in that region. There is evidence that God is opening a similar window of opportunity in the Muslim world.

Even the tragedy of war might prove a turning point for the Gulf region. Change and upheaval often result in openness, and no one is expecting the Arab states of the region to return to the way they were before August 1990. Osama Baz, a senior advisor to Egypt's president Mubarak, said, "We are certain that, in the aftermath of the earthquake, the Arab world will never be the same."[3] What the new order might look like is a matter of speculation, but there are hopeful signs and some wide-open opportunities.

The government of Kuwait was signing contracts for between $50 billion and $100 billion worth of reconstruction, even before the shooting had stopped. Over the next several years, the American and other foreign companies who have those contracts will be hiring people with all kinds of skills, including tentmakers with an interest in the Muslim world. Another door is open for ministries of compassion to meet the physical needs of people displaced and traumatized by the war, including refugees.

The very presence of half a million American troops in the region may have unforeseen consequences. During the military buildup, there were reports of numerous conversions among the troops. Jesus Christ was being worshiped in small gatherings in tents in a land where Christian worship of any kind has been stringently outlawed. Even more significant than this spiritual foothold is the impact those service men and women might have over time. After World War 2, there was a tremendous surge of missionary interest among returning veterans who had seen the world and who spearheaded new mission thrusts into Europe, Japan and the Pacific. The same commitment to return to the Gulf as messengers of the Prince of Peace might take hold of young people who have spent months in an Islamic country and, in some cases, fought side-by-side with Muslim soldiers.

God Is at Work

Whatever the response of the church in the West to the needs of people in the 10/40 window, there are signs that God is already at work, intervening in supernatural ways in people's lives.

Bill Musk, a long-time missionary in Egypt, reports the story of a Muslim woman living in southern Thailand who had a vision in which Christ appeared to her and healed her crippled limbs. She was then given instructions to travel ten miles north to find a man she saw in another vision. The man gave her a Bible, and she became a believer. In a village in Algeria, almost every adult was visited by the Lord in a dream or vision one night. They woke up and began to tell each other what they had seen, quickly realizing that virtually everyone had had the same experience. Three hundred villagers became believers in Jesus that day. An Arab Christian got wind of this and decided to investigate. To his amazement he discovered that during the 13th century the missionary Raymond Lull had been martyred in that very village—a rather dramatic demonstration that the blood of the martyrs is indeed the seed of the church.

In 1973, tentmaker Christie Wilson was preparing to leave Afghanistan, where he had ministered to many blind people. As he prayed for the people he was leaving behind, God gave him a promise from Isaiah 42:16, "I will lead the blind by ways they have not known, along unfamiliar paths I will guide them; I will turn the darkness into light before them and make the rough places smooth."

More than fifteen years later one of the leaders of the church in Kabul, a blind man who had been led to the Lord by another tentmaker, Dwight Ritchie, was captured by Muslim fundamentalists and taken behind rebel lines. His captors had begun to torture him, when suddenly there was an explosion outside the building, and he was able to escape. He walked for mile after mile along paths and roads, past military checkpoints, all the way back to Kabul, and he returned to the marketplace and began to preach the Gospel. God's promise had been fulfilled.

In another Muslim country, a devastating drought threatened the livelihoods of poor farmers. In one village the Muslim holy men stood in the fields day after day, praying for Allah to send rain to save the crops. When there was no rain, they went to a Christian couple living in the village and said, "We have prayed to God, but he does not answer. Please pray to your God to send rain."

The Christians went into the fields to pray, determined to stay there until the rain came. For two hours they prayed, and the villagers laughed. Then suddenly, a few small clouds began to appear, then more as the wind picked up and the sky darkened. Torrents of life-giving rain poured down, and the villagers ran from house to house shouting, "Their God answers prayer!"

That Christian couple had been trained to share the good news with Muslims. They had a culturally sensitive translation of the Bible in the language of the people. And as a result of the miraculous intervention of God and the faithful witness of such couples, there are thousands of baptized families gathered into several hundred congregations in the villages of that region.

How Will We Respond?

These hints at the beginning of a time of harvest in the least-evangelized part of the world prompt an important question:

How will the church around the world respond to this *kairos* opportunity?

There are many sad examples of missed opportunity in history. Centuries ago Kublai Khan, then ruler of the Mongol Empire covering most of Asia, asked Christians to send emissaries. After a number of years, two semi-literate priests arrived in Mongolia, but even they didn't stay for long. In the wake of World War 2, General Douglas MacArthur recognized the tremendous spiritual need of the Japanese people and issued a call for missionaries. Few responded. During the 1980s the Soviet invasion forced more than five million Afghan refugees into Pakistan, a country much more accessible to Christian witness. Despite some attempts to reach out to the refugees, the church failed to mobilize the resources needed to take advantage of the opportunity.

The urgent needs of people living in the 10/40 window and the hopeful signs of spiritual change there challenge Christians to find ways of bringing the gospel to the creative access world. Countries that are not interested in "missionaries" often open their doors to teachers, health-care workers, engineers and businesspeople. By providing a service the country needs and wants, tentmakers have the opportunity to build relationships with neighbors and coworkers.

Even in countries where missionaries are allowed, tentmakers can make a unique contribution—as the story of Gladys Aylward proves. Gladys Aylward was convinced that God wanted her to minister to the Chinese people, and when the mission board turned her down, she saved her money and bought a train ticket.

She started out in late 1932, traveling through a war zone to join an elderly lady who ran an inn for the muleteers who transported goods across China's countryside. She worked with her partner, Mrs. Lawson, providing the muleteers clean rooms, good food, and stories from God's Word. Their reputation grew, but when Mrs. Lawson died and the subsidy she had been receiving from England stopped, the inn was about to go under.

A visit from the local Mandarin solved Gladys's financial problems. The government had just ordered that all women's feet be unbound, but custom dictated that a Chinese man could not inspect a woman's feet. Gladys was the only woman in the province with unbound feet, and she was offered the job of traveling through the province to enforce the new decree. She accepted—on the condition that she be allowed to tell her Bible stories as she went from house to house.

Today's tentmaker in China, as in many other places, is more likely to be an English teacher than an "inspector of feet," but the principle of building friendships and sharing stories remains unchanged.

Mark, a young man from Ohio, inexplicably felt God say, "Go to China and teach English." He went on faith, and finally began to understand why God had called him when one of his students approached him after class.

Zhang, an engineering student who was studying English in order to have access to the latest technical journals and Western research, had begun to question the Marxist promise of an ideal society built on materialism and socialism. But he couldn't discuss his doubts with his classmates because a note in his student records about his doubts might damage his career.

He asked Mark, "Do you think that knowledge is enough to help us in China?"

Mark was ready for that question. He began with Solomon's words "The fear of the Lord is the beginning of knowledge" and proceeded to lead Zhang into a relationship with the Lord.

Shifting Missionary Resources

The challenge of the creative access world demands a reallocation of resources in world mission. About fifteen years ago, mission strategists began pointing out that current mission efforts were overlooking many groups of people that were "unreached," having no viable witness within their culture or language.

Something like 90 per cent of the mission force was working with existing churches and basically evangelized groups of people, leaving only a few workers for pioneering situations. During the past decade, new agencies with names like "Frontiers" and "Pioneers" have sprung up, while other missions have reexamined their priorities and targeted specific unreached groups.

Still, the overall picture hasn't changed much. Of the more than 40,000 North American evangelical missionaries serving overseas, only about thirteen per cent serve in the countries of the 10/40 window. Of that small group, more than half of them are in Indonesia and Japan[4] (and most of the missionaries in Indonesia work with the one per cent of the population that is tribal). The need to reallocate missionary resources to the most needy parts of the world—and to the most strategically important—is still urgent.

One local church in the Northwest is taking this call seriously. A number of years ago the mission department decided to allocate more resources to the neediest part of the world. They wanted twenty-five per cent of their overseas mission resources to support people and projects working with Muslims. Reaching that goal has meant tough decisions to cut back in other areas, but they want their limited resources to count in strategic areas. Finding those ministries has stretched the church's vision. One mission committee member says, "More and more members of the congregation have begun to be aware of this great area of need, and are not just giving up on it."

Perhaps even more encouraging than the efforts of individual churches and mission agencies is the way that God is raising up a whole new force in world mission—missionaries from the non-Western world. According to Luis Bush, non-Western missionaries will outnumber Western missionaries by the year 2000. Most of this new mission effort is focused on church planting and evangelism, especially among unreached people groups. Bush heads Partners International, an agency dedicated to encouraging and supporting indigenous mission organizations around the world. He describes Third World missionaries in this way: "They are newer to the faith, they have a vibrancy, a sense of the fullness of the Spirit. They have a high level of faith, they're high risk takers."

India has the greatest number of missionaries, most of whom work in the northern part of the country where Islam and Hinduism have the strongest hold on people. South Korean churches have already placed missionaries in 64 countries, primarily in Asia, but plan to have workers in the remaining nations by 2000.

Throughout Latin America, new mission structures are springing up, with a special emphasis on Arab peoples. A Muslim-ministry training center has been set up in Spain to train Latin American workers, and a goal has been set to place one hundred missionaries in Arab countries by 2000. These workers hope to use affinities between Latin and Arab cultures that were forged during 800 years of Moorish occupation of Spain to build bridges for the gospel. The Moors were forced out of Spain about the time Columbus arrived in the Americas, so the Spanish culture that has taken root in the New World is heavily influenced by the Arabic. One strategist has pointed out there are 6,000 words that are nearly the same in Spanish and Arabic, and concepts of time and hospitality are also similar.

Luis Bush tells of meeting a leader of a multinational Operation Mobilization team working in a Muslim country. The most effective person on the team, he was told, was a Brazilian woman.

The 10/40 window helps us see major areas where the gospel hasn't yet been proclaimed, and it challenges us to focus our resources strategically on the remaining task. Yet the picture isn't a gloomy one—there are indications of new opportunities throughout the region, and a mobilization of people and resources throughout the world. This is also another place to look for hope, a *kairos* moment in progress that helps us to anticipate the surprising ways God might begin to work in the 10/40 window.

Questions for Groups or Individuals

1. The 10/40 window represents a great correlation of spiritual and physical needs. How can the hope of Christ address both aspects of need?

2. Do you think ministry to one of these needs is more important than the other? Explain.

3. Discuss the impact of the Gulf War on the task of evangelizing that region. What needs and opportunities have been revealed?

What difficulties do you see?

4. What skills do you have or are you training for that might qualify you to work in another country as a tentmaker?

5. How can you begin to learn about another culture, particularly one representing the 10/40 window? (Are there interna-

tional students on your campus or immigrant enclaves in your city? Look for ethnic restaurants, stores or places of worship.)

For Further Study
Urbana Tapes
Plenary Session Video #1, *God So Loved the World,* Mary Fisher.
Plenary Session Video #2, *Colossians 2: Lordship of Christ,* Luis Bush.
Plenary Session Video #3, *Branching Out,* George Otis, Jr.
Audio #7189, "Hope for the Creative Access World," George Otis, Jr.

Bible Studies
Aeschliman, Gordon. *Leadership in the 21st Century.* Global Issues Bible Studies. Downers Grove, Ill.: InterVarsity Press, 1990.
Truman, Bryan. *Basic Human Needs.* Global Issues Bible Studies. Downers Grove, Ill.: InterVarsity Press, 1990.
Webb, Jana L. *Economic Justice.* Global Issues Bible Studies. Downers Grove, Ill.: InterVarsity Press, 1990.

Books
Aeschliman, Gordon. *GlobalTrends.* Downers Grove, Ill.: InterVarsity Press, 1990. Ten trends that Christians must respond to in the world.
Hale, Thomas. *On the Far Side of Liglig Mountain.* Grand Rapids, Mich.: Zondervan, 1989. The ministry of a medical missionary in Nepal.
Hamilton, Don. *Tentmakers Speak.* Ventura, Calif: Regal, 1988. A practical look at ministry in the creative access world.

6

God's Day for Eastern Europe

I n 1988, the Soviet government proclaimed the success of their educational system by quoting surveys that showed about 90 per cent of young people between sixteen and twenty years old accepted atheism as their world view. Just two years later, a Soviet sociologist summarized his research as indicating that at least 80 per cent of the Soviet population could be characterized as spiritual seekers.

The sudden demise of Marxist ideology in Eastern Europe and the Soviet Union, symbolized by the dismantling of the Berlin Wall, has revealed a spiritual hunger that is just as real as the hunger for political freedom and economic opportunity that toppled governments at the end of 1989. Peter Kuzmic, who has been training Eastern European pastors for many years at the Evangelical Theological Seminary in Osijek, Yugoslavia, describes the changes in the region this way: "The Lord is the Lord of the harvest, but he is also the Lord of history. And he has just decided to rearrange history in Eastern Europe so that we can have an unprecedented harvest before his return."

Eastern Europe is experiencing a *kairos* moment—through the tumultuous events of 1989 God is flinging wide the doors of opportunity.

Filling the Spiritual Void

Outside of Bratislava, Czechoslovakia, there is a forest littered with the statues and symbols of the former Communist regimes, hammers and sickles lying next to the enormous bronze bust of Lenin that used to stand in the middle of the city. Students call the place "the village of the ridiculous."

All over Eastern Europe town squares have been emptied of their monuments. In many cases the statues disappeared overnight without a word. The empty pedestals symbolize the region's precarious position. The old icons have been removed, but what will fill the moral and spiritual void of these societies?

It's a question being asked by many people in the region. Some of Eastern Europe's new leaders met at Northwestern University in March 1990 to discuss where the revolution in Europe was headed. Romania's ambassador to the United Nations characterized their discussion by saying, "When you live in a moral void for 45 years, the basic need is a society based on morality." With the ideological underpinnings of their societies discredited, people are looking for something to base their lives on.

Anita Deyneka, who heads up the Slavic Gospel Association's Institute of Soviet and East European Studies, met Dr. Mikhail Matskovsky at a conference on Slavic Studies. Matskovsky, a sociologist affiliated with the Soviet Academy of Scientists, has been working on a project to research the awareness of the Ten Commandments in Soviet society. "He said he was interested in the subject because he thought Marxism had failed to provide an ethical basis for society," says Deyneka.

Matskovsky's other research had led him to the conclusion that the Bible was the book most desired by Soviet people, and that about 80 per cent of the population could be characterized as spiritual seekers. One Russian who came upon a New Testament "by chance" expressed his reaction to reading it in a letter that was published in a popular Russian magazine:

> I just turned over the last page of a great book and I'm overcome with feelings of gratitude and happiness. But there are some bitter questions that have remained unanswered. Why only now? Who decided, and on what grounds, that this book was harmful to me? In our time of unrest and brokenness, when crystal palaces turn out to be cardboard shacks, when once majestic kings are now covered with shame, when under the granite edifices are unstable foundations of clay, then I know that there is a book to which I can always return, and it will help comfort and support me in the darkest hour.

Anita Deyneka reported that her recent travels in the Soviet Union confirm an unprecedented level of interest in spiritual things. "On every level of society from the higher party schools to taxi drivers, people are searching for spiritual meaning to replace their disillusionment with Marxist ideology," says Anita. "I find increasingly that it's eclectic, with Eastern thought and New Age ideas. They aren't necessarily searching for Christianity."

A Christian Presence

The church, of course, has not been absent for the past decades.

"We never gave up hope under communism," says Peter Kuzmic. "We knew that communism was wrong when they said that the church would disappear, that there would be no need for religion because they were building a new society. This was an inner conviction within us, an inner spark of hope."

That hope was most clearly and dramatically evident in the witness of Christians in the face of persecution. In the Siberian city of Barnaul, members of the Baptist Church suffered on-going harassment and persecution after they refused to accept a government-appointed pastor in 1961. Yet they clung to their faith and their fellowship, and their love couldn't be contained. When one of the atheist agitators in town fell seriously ill, they visited him in the hospital. He told them, "You believers don't leave the dying without comfort. That is your secret. My own comrades haven't visited me once. And you always bring gifts along besides!"[1]

By the time Galina Vilchinskaya was 26, she had spent nearly five years in Soviet prisons and camps. She was arrested the first time for helping to organize a camp for the children of prisoners. Though the terrible conditions of the Gulag nearly destroyed her health, she saw a larger purpose in her sufferings. "I feel that I won't last long here. But it doesn't matter. I rejoice. They are providing me the opportunity to evangelize my camp, and more people can hear about the Lord. . . . I'm needed here more than in freedom. So many starving, suffering outcasts are here."[2]

Holding on to hope means seeing opportunity in the midst of difficulty. Peter Kuzmic points to St. Augustine's notion that hope has two daughters, anger and courage—anger with the way things are and the courage to change them. "One has to do with your dissatisfaction with the status of things. The other is your involvement on behalf of Christ and his kingdom."

In countries like Yugoslavia, where there was relatively more religious freedom, Christians like Peter Kuzmic have been able to demonstrate the viability of faith in other ways. Over the past decade, he was involved in formulating a Christian response to Marxism, dialoguing with a number of Marxist scholars. "There was always a certain anger with the way they distorted the dream they had about a new society, but I was never on an anticommunist crusade. I always saw the Marxist communists as people—they are lovable, redeemable human beings."

Peter's willingness to engage in dialog with the theorists of Marxism gave him some unique opportunities to tell them about Christ. On one occasion he addressed the prime minister, the president and vice president of Yugoslavia at a reception. "I told them there is no hope for the country without the moral and spiritual renewal of the society. I asked them to read the Good Book and to take seriously Jesus Christ, the only person who ever walked this planet who never lied, never stole, never had an evil motive in his heart, where we see a perfect harmony of theory and practice, word and deed. I asked them to look at his life and respond to his program."

Christians Involved in Change

Not only are there churches and faithful Christians who endured various attempts to undermine religion, in some instances these Christians have played key roles in helping their countries to shake off the old system. The people of Romania suffered tremendously under the cruel dictatorship of Ceaucescu, but at the same time, Romania has been a land of great revival. Ceaucescu remained in power even after most of the other Communist regimes in the region had fallen, until a crowd of people gathered to protect a pastor who was about to be evicted from his parish because of his criticism of the regime.

Eventually the crowd swelled and filled the main square of Timisoara, close to 200,000 people gathering between the old Orthodox Cathedral and the National Theater. While the secret police were still trying to fight against the crowd, speakers on the balcony of the theater addressed the crowd. One of them, an evangelical pastor, said, "I am a preacher of the gospel. The Securitate [secret police] tried to kill me also, but they could not. For over 40 years they told us that God does not exist, but God exists." The crowd took up his words in a chant, "God exists. God exists." When he could get their attention again, he said, "Let us pray." The crowd dropped to their knees, and he led them in the Lord's Prayer.

Today, according to Peter Kuzmic, Timisoara is "the most evangelical city in Europe," and the Timisoara Theological Institute is the largest evangelical seminary on the continent. Romanian Christians are having an impact on the nation.

The changes in Eastern Europe, while they bring a hope for freedom and opportunity, have brought their own forms of turmoil and pain. The change from centrally planned economies to a market system has caused real suffering, as evidenced by the Soviet Union's request for outside aid to help feed its people. Old ethnic rivalries and nationalistic feelings are threatening the new democracies of Eastern Europe and the progress of reform in the Soviet Union. Peter Kuzmic calls Christians "a factor of stability" in the midst of these challenges. "People very often trust evangelical Christians more than they trust anybody else because they know these people are honest. They don't have selfish ambitions and interests. They aren't going to manipulate people for their own purposes."

Philemon Choi took some students from Hong Kong to learn from the experience of the church in Eastern Europe. "To our amazement," he reports, "Christians in these countries were instrumental in bringing hope to the whole nation. They were the people who offered truth when truth could not be heard in the country." They visited a Polish church where the pastor had been nicknamed "Protector." Philemon explains, "During times of persecution, sometimes they had a really hard time, but he offered shelter for those who were persecuted. People just flocked into the church." The integrity of Christians during times when it was costly to profess faith in Christ has not gone unnoticed. In Yugoslavia, ethnic tensions are accentuated by the religious affiliations of the various nationalities—Serbs are traditionally Orthodox, while Croatians are mostly Catholic. Kuzmic says the evangelicals are being asked to contribute to the new order, "to reflect on the situation and provide a biblical, holistic answer to the problems. They know that we are not Christians out of nationalism or out of our history. We are Christians out of conviction."

Kuzmic gave a newspaper interview in late 1990, and of the wide range of topics covered, the editors chose one simple statement to run as the headline: "God is not a nationalist." Kuzmic explains, "We were saying that we would not allow secular politicians to divide us as the body of Christ, because we have one Lord."

In Yugoslavia's southern province of Kosovo, tensions between Serbs and the approximately two million Albanians who live there run very high, occasionally sparking violent outbursts. But in the midst of the tensions, Anton Krasnici is known as a reconciler. He was an Albanian lawyer who became a Christian and now pastors the first Albanian church anywhere in the world. Even while the Communists were still in power, he was invited to appear on the radio alongside a secular psychologist, answering people's questions on a live call-in show. "He's building bridges between the different nationalities in the region," says Kuzmic.

Responding to Spiritual Need

Although the spiritual openness is great, there are some parts of the region where the church may not be prepared to respond to the opportunities. Anita Deyneka describes the Soviet evangelical church as "strong, vital, valiant, purified," but points out that their numbers may be even smaller than some Western observers have believed. There are many testimonies of incredible faithfulness through years of very harsh persecution, where people witnessed in prison and started churches in the places they were exiled, yet much of the church is culturally cut off from the society at large.

"In many ways it is not well-prepared to take advantage of the openness in society and the people reaching out for spiritual help from every side," Deyneka explains. "Inevitably this will change as society becomes less hostile and antagonistic, and as they are able to participate in areas of society where they have been excluded before, especially education and the media."

But Soviet Christians aren't waiting to respond to the needs of their country. The first nationwide mission conference was held in November 1989, bringing together pastors, evangelists and lay leaders from seventy-five cities. During the conference, delegates shared reports of new mission efforts to reach remote parts of the country as well as ministries to the urban masses, even serving as volunteers in psychiatric hospitals. In October 1990, a conference on evangelism in Moscow drew one thousand Soviet Christians, and much of the emphasis was on the un-evangelized parts of the country, including the republics where 55 million Muslims live.

Anita Deyneka met some of those involved in pioneering efforts. She says, "I know Christians who are moving from Russian areas to live as tentmakers in the Muslim republics. Others are evangelists. They gave up their jobs and are living by faith as they visit churches and minister."

Western Involvement

There are exciting opportunities for Christians from the West to participate in God's *kairos* moment for Eastern Europe and the Soviet Union. The easiest way to enter the Soviet Union is as a student. For several years teams of InterVarsity students have participated in an educational and cultural exchange pro-gram with Soviet students in Kiev and other cities.

In 1990, 800 Soviet students applied for twenty-five places in the Kiev program. Nikki was one of those twenty-five. "I wanted to participate in this program because I knew that the Americans would be Christians," she says. "Ever since I was young I thought that there must be a God, but I couldn't find anyone to tell me in ways I could understand."

Nikki and her fellow students shared dorm rooms, meals, classes, outings and even Bible study and worship times with the American students in the program. Through their develop-ing friendships, she found the chance to ask the questions she had about God.

"I asked so many questions," she says. "Like, 'Where is heav-en?' 'Why is Jesus the only way?' and 'How do you know it's true?' " Her American friends did their best to answer them.

By the end of the first week of the program, Nikki had given her life to Jesus. Some of her Soviet friends told her she would stop believing after the Americans left, but about half of the Soviet participants had also become Christians and their fellowship proved a source of strength.

"Even though I was very sad that August, I still felt this feeling of hope. I had never felt hope like this before in my life. It made me keep reading the Bible and praying to God—it was like I couldn't help doing these things."

Today there is a fellowship of Christian students and faculty meeting in Kiev, and the seeds of a Christian student movement are being nurtured in other cities as well. The opportunities to influence the future leaders of the region with the message of hope seem wide open, but the task is urgent. Political and economic turmoil in the Soviet Union and some of the other Eastern European countries may limit access, and Christians are not the only ones rushing to fill the spiritual void.

Between the summer of 1990 and the end of 1991, members of the Unification Church of Rev. Sun Myung Moon expect to have brought 3,000 Soviet students to the United States for sightseeing and lectures on Moon's doctrine.[3] Representatives of the Moonie church advertise the free trips on campuses and have approached university administrators, asking specifically to be introduced to students who have had contact with Christian groups.

Seven of the Soviet students who participated in the Kiev InterVarsity project accepted the invitation to attend a conference in New York. One of the Soviet students had become a Christian during the previous summer, and two others had accepted Christ since then. A fourth became a believer during their time in New York, according to some of their American friends who were able to visit the Soviets in New York.

The conference sparked intense discussions on the differences between the faith lived out by Christian believers and the Moonies. At the end of the conference, all seven refused to sign the commitment card. Having seen the reality of Christ in their friends' lives, they could recognize the counterfeit faith. Unfortunately, few of their compatriots have seen such a clear witness to the truth.

Questions for Groups or Individuals

1. Does the church of Jesus Christ depend on political freedom for its life and ministry? Explain.

2. What can we learn from the experience of Christians in Eastern Europe and the Soviet Union during times of restriction and repression?

3. What new opportunities for evangelism and mission have arisen with the changes in the Eastern Bloc?

4. What new threats to the growth of the church may be present?

5. How might you, your church or your fellowship get involved in Eastern Europe or the Soviet Union?

6. How might the example of a *kairos* moment for Eastern Europe and the Soviet Union apply to other parts of the world—for example, the Persian Gulf or China?

7. How might this change the way you pray for the world?

For Further Study
Urbana Tapes
Plenary Session Video #3, *Branching Out,* Anita Deyneka.
Plenary Session Video #7, *Students in World Mission,* Peter

Kuzmic.

Audio #7189, "Students in Creative Access Countries," Anita Deyneka.

Audio #7191, "Call to Commitment," Peter Kuzmic.

Audio #7433, "Global Revolutions and Christian Relief and Development," Amy Sherman.

Books

Deyneka, Anita and Peter, Jr. *A Song in Siberia.* Elgin, Ill.: David C. Cook, 1977. A powerful account of the church's endurance.

Posterski, Don. *Reinventing Evangelism.* Downers Grove, Ill.: InterVarsity Press, 1989. How to present the gospel in a changing world.

Study Programs

For information on study and exchange programs in Eastern Europe and the Soviet Union, contact:

Global Projects, InterVarsity Missions, P.O. Box 7895, Madison, Wis. 53707 (608/274-9001).

Institute of Eastern European Studies, Slavic Gospel Association, P.O. Box 1122, Wheaton, Ill. 60189 (708/690-8900).

7

The Challenge
of the Cities

I saac Canales, pastor of the Misión Eben-Ezer Family Church, met Patrick one hot Saturday morning. Patrick and other members of his gang—a Filipino gang related to Los Angeles' infamous "Bloods"—were gathered across from Isaac's house, writing their gang name on a fence. "I could tell they were up all night long," Isaac explains, "so I got a pitcher of punch and took it out to them. They drank it, and then I said, 'Why don't you go somewhere else?' "

A couple of days later, Isaac was driving home when he saw Patrick walking along, looking dejected and wearing the same clothes he had on the other day. Isaac slowed down and started a conversation. "What's happening, man? You look real bummed out."

"Oh, you don't want to hear it," Patrick replied.

"Yeah, I do want to hear it. Get in the car."

"No, I'm all messed up."

"Get in the car," Isaac insisted. "Are you hungry?"

Isaac took Patrick to a local burger place, ordered food, and talked while the boy ate. "I started to share with him what I knew about the kind of life he was leading and where that was going to end up—which was basically being killed or being incarcerated for a long time. As I was talking to him, the Lord was ministering to him, and he was crying. His tears were falling in his ketchup, making a mess. I said, 'Listen, would you like to give your life to the Lord?' So he gave his heart to Christ."

Isaac learned that Patrick had been living on the streets for the past eight months. A few days later, Isaac and his wife, Retha, decided they wanted to take a chance on Patrick and invited him to stay in their home. "It was really hard," Isaac recalls, "because he was rough around the edges. His father died in the Philippines when he was six. His mom disowned him when he was fourteen. He had no discipline whatsoever. If you tried to hug him, he'd jerk away."

It wasn't easy for him to make a break from the gang, either. "While he was at our home, he was stabbed. Then, he was shot in the back. And we'd run to the hospital to see what's going on. When he was shot, I refused to go see him, because all his friends were there, and he was becoming a hero of his gang. So I said, 'Go tell Patrick when he gets out, we'll talk.'"

Patrick stayed with the Canales family for a year, and now is living with a Christian Filipino family.

Not too long after Patrick moved out, Isaac opened his front door to find a fourteen-year-old gang member, a friend of Patrick's, camped out on his front step. He said to Isaac, "Pastor, where do I go? I ran away from home. My stepfather don't love me; my mother don't want me." And so the cycle began again.

"Our ministry is dealing with people one to one," Isaac explains. "If they're a leader, like Patrick, and God does a mighty work, that confuses the whole gang. We're not out to confuse the gang, we're out to win one kid. Whatever happens after that, that's just part of what Christ does."

Hopelessness in the City

Gang violence in American cities has taken on frightening dimensions in the past few years as the drug trade and increasingly vicious weapons claim more and more victims. Between 1985 and 1990, the number of gangs and gang members in Los Angeles County doubled. In 1990 there were more than 600 gang-related deaths. Washington, D.C., has been labeled the murder capital of the country. For the third year in a row a record-breaking number of homicides occurred there.

Violence is just one symptom of the hopelessness that haunts our cities. There are three million homeless people in the United States, more than a third of them families with children. Unemployment for black teens was 35 per cent at the end of 1990. The inferior educational systems and depressed environments of the inner city reinforce the hopelessness experienced by many young people.

"You grow up in a situation where the question is stated, 'Will you ever amount to anything? Will you ever succeed?' " says Glandion Carney, who grew up in Oakland, California.

The Source of Hope

Glandion found hope through the friendship of a high-school

teacher named Kenneth Jenson. "It was in the 1960s when White people were highly suspected by Blacks. As a White man, Kenneth Jenson was also suspected, but he came into the community with a servant's heart and a commitment to demonstrate the message of Christ. He spent time with us, took us to Youth For Christ rallies. He was a friend, a supporter, a brother." Through Kenneth's influence, Glandion accepted Christ and began to discover the hope of living out the love of Christ.

"In the inner city there are lots of images of failure," says Glandion, "what I call the visible manifestations of evil, things like drugs and poverty. Urban ministry has to be holistic, it has to bring visible grace." Glandion believes that visible grace comes when Christians come alongside urban dwellers and work with them on their needs.

For a child who might drop out of school because she can't read, tutoring is a manifestation of grace. For refugees bewildered by a new language and a strange environment, teaching English and offering practical skills demonstrates hope. Working with city dwellers to repair dilapidated housing or improve the physical appearance of the community can be a way to incarnate Christ's love too. Glandion says, "I'm convinced that is part of what grace is."

Bob LaVelle's commitment to the Pittsburgh neighborhood where he grew up manifests hope in another form. A number of years ago, he scraped together $67,000 to begin Dwelling House Savings and Loan. He makes home loans to poor families who might not qualify for mortgages from regular banks because their homes are in areas considered too risky for the banks to invest in.

Dwelling House works to help its clients succeed—teaching money management and offering free financial counseling.

Many of Bob's clients have moved off the welfare rolls, developed skills, found jobs and now own their own homes. They have a stake in their community, and a voice to complain about how their taxes are spent or to influence their children's education. They have a hope that they wouldn't have if Bob La-Velle hadn't responded to Jesus' call to care for the poor.

Even in the most desperate situations, people who have the hope of Christ can make a difference. A woman approached Glandion Carney and asked him to visit her son, who was in the hospital. When Glandion inquired about her son's condition, she hesitated, obviously embarrassed and afraid. "My son has AIDS," she said.

Glandion found the young man curled up in his hospital bed in the fetal position. He weighed about 90 pounds, and his hair was falling out. He was barely conscious. Glandion saw why his mother had wanted this man to experience some kind of comfort, some kind of hope. "I took the young man's hand, and I prayed for him and read him some psalms, and I kissed his brow," he says. Two days later he died, but the mother knew that her son had experienced hope.

"You bring hope when you touch someone who isn't being touched," says Glandion. "When we take on the cross of Christ and the message of Christ, we are living incarnations of faith. Our presence is the presence of Christ."

The City Cries Out

Some of the characteristics of cities that make them so evidently in need of the gospel also make them strategic targets of mission effort. Within the next decade, for the first time in human history, more than half the world's people will live in urban areas. As urban pastor Tom Wolfe puts it, "The distinctive of our generation is global urbanization."

Cities are mushrooming all around the world, and the ones in the Two-Thirds World are growing the fastest. Mexico City is the largest city in the world, with nineteen million people. The city is growing by a million people each year—a combination of high birth rates and continuing migration from rural areas. Mexico City contains a quarter of the country's population and a disproportionate share of industry, jobs and investment.

As it drains resources from the rest of the country, it continues to draw people by the thousands, most of whom will live in squatter communities—hillsides covered with shacks of all descriptions, crowding together with little or no sanitation or clean water. Underground aquifers are being drained to quench the city's growing thirst at such a rate that some parts of the city are sinking by twelve inches a year.[1]

For example, Mexico City is built on a high plateau at 7,500 feet and surrounded by mountains. At that altitude the air has only half the oxygen present at sea level, and the mountains trap pollutants. The city is scrambling to solve its smog problems by mandating that drivers keep their cars at home one day a week.

Mexico City's story is repeated hundreds of times around the globe. By 2000 eight of the ten largest cities will be in the developing countries and will include São Paulo, Shanghai, Bombay, Calcutta and Jakarta. According to Viv Grigg, an urban church planter now coordinating the AD 2000 Movement's urban track, the last forty years saw a billion people migrate into cities. The next decade may well see another billion urban migrants.

Already, seventeen per cent of the world's population lives in urban slums or squatter areas. Cities around the world are creating new jobs at only half the rate needed to keep up with the number of people pouring into them. The dreams of new opportunities that migrants bring with them to the city fade fast.

The realities of life for these people are grim. In most cities there are entire cultures that have grown up around the garbage dumps. Children are born on the dumps. They spend their days, not in school, but scavenging through piles of garbage for items that can be sold to help support their families.

In Calcutta, millions of people live on the streets. Generations live and die without ever having a roof over their heads. It is estimated that two-thirds of Calcutta's people live in extreme poverty. In Addis Ababa, some 90 per cent of the people live in slums.[2]

The powerless and voiceless of the urban slums fall prey to exploitation of all kinds. There are 500,000 child prostitutes in Bangkok.[3] In many cities beggars are controlled by middle men who take the lion's share of their earnings. Other city dwellers are simply lost, like the pack of preteen boys missionary Rick Johnson found living in an abandoned building in Tijuana, Mexico. They spend their days sniffing glue, the drug of choice for kids with no money and no hope.

But as overwhelming as the desperate cry of the urban world is, God's words to Jonah echo across centuries: "But Nineveh has more than a hundred and twenty thousand people who cannot tell their right hand from their left, and many cattle as well. Should I not be concerned about that great city?" (Jon 4:11). Indeed, as urban missiologists point out, God is very concerned for the cities of our world. In the words of Ray Bakke, "The story of salvation begins in a garden (Gen 1), and ends in a city (Rev 22)."[4]

A Place for Mission

The rapid urbanization of our world has many strategic implications for mission efforts aimed at evangelizing not only the
urban masses, but the whole world. Primary cities are ones
which act as centers for culture, political power and economic
development—often they set the tone for an entire nation. Bue-
nos Aires, for example, has about one-third of Argentina's
population, but more than 80 per cent of the country's tele-
phones. One-third of the economic product of India passes
through Bombay.

Cities are places of diversity, bringing together people of different nationalities, languages, cultures and religions.

For Isaac Canales, the world lives right next door, and the
membership of his bilingual church reflects the diversity of his
Los Angeles neighborhood. The Spanish-language service in-
cludes people from almost every country in Latin America, plus
Spain. "On the English-speaking side, we have Samoan, Filipi-
no, Chinese, Hawaiian, Vietnamese," says Isaac. "Then we have
African-Americans, Anglo-Americans and English-speaking
Hispanics."

Los Angeles is one of the new gateways of immigration.
Public-school students there speak more than 100 different
languages at home. The Mexicans and Mexican-Americans in
Los Angeles by themselves would form the second-largest city
in Mexico. The same is true for Vietnamese, Filipinos, Koreans,
Guatemalans and Salvadorans. When the Soviet Union began
to relax its restrictions on immigration in the late 1980s, Armenians headed for Los Angeles by the tens of thousands.

The cultural diversity of cities offers the possibility of reaching people groups from the "creative access" world. Unfortunately, like many other forms of urban ministry, this opportu-

nity is often overlooked by the church. The cities of Western Europe are home to six million Muslims, and yet relatively few efforts are being made to share the gospel with them, away from the legal restrictions of their countries of origin in North Africa, the Middle East or Asia.[4] In British cities, areas populated by immigrants have largely been abandoned by Christians, and many empty churches have been converted into mosques.

Tom Wolfe points out the importance of cities for evangelization: "Cities are ripe for the gospel. Country people are more closed. Urban people are accustomed to outsiders—they are receptive to other ideas. The city is influential, for every person in the city has a relative in the smaller towns and villages. If you start churches there, other people who know the culture can take it to the people in the hinterland."

Calcutta, for example, has 85 distinct people groups. The largest, about eight million strong, is the Bengali people, who represent one of the largest unreached people groups in the world—fifty million between Bangladesh and India. "To reach the Bengalis," says Viv Grigg, "you have to reach Calcutta." There are a handful of Bengali-language churches in Calcutta, but only one in the slums *(bustees)*.

The Key to the City

According to Viv, church-planting movements are the key to reaching cities. Over the next few years, the AD 2000 Movement will be helping churches and missions worldwide to network and strategize to reach the 1,000 least-evangelized cities. The goal is to have at least one church-planting movement among the poor, and another among the educated elite, probably beginning with a student movement.

Reaching the poor is key, in that they represent the greatest numbers, and frequently the greatest receptivity to the gospel. Viv believes that recent migrants are most open to accept Christ during their first ten years in the city.

Evangelizing those who will one day be leaders in government, business and the professions represents the greatest hope for justice for the poor. Calcutta, for example, has more than 100 universities, but there is no evangelical student ministry group active on those campuses today. "If they have a holistic theology related to the poor, we find it begins to transform the structures of society which oppress the poor," says Viv.

Not surprisingly, many of these least-evangelized cities will be found within the 10/40 window. Manila, where Viv first experienced God's call to identify with the poorest of the poor and share the message of hope through an incarnational witness, had only three churches in the slums in 1978. Now there are 51—for three million squatters.

In contrast, urban churches are growing among the poor in Latin American cities. When Viv travelled to Brazil to share his burden for the urban poor, Brazilian Christians caught the vision immediately. Out of that encounter has grown an indigenous Brazilian mission called "Servants among the Poor," which has established church-planting teams in Lima, Bogota, North Africa and hopes to have one in Mexico City by the end of 1991.

What does hope look like in an urban slum in the Two-Thirds World? Luis Bush visited a community of dedicated servants who minister to the 7,000 people who live on Manila's dump. The team was made up of about twenty persons, more than half of them Filipinos, the others representing six other countries. They had established a program to feed young children, and some were trained in community health care. "While

I was there they were preparing a room that was to be used as a Christian pre-school," recalls Luis. A church had been started and some fourteen Bible study groups met in various homes throughout the community.

Hope had broken through the despair of poverty, and Luis could observe the signs of that hope. What impressed him most was something a young man named Andrew said to him as they watched children picking cans and bottles out of the garbage: "These are beautiful people. It is a privilege to work here."

Cities are not beautiful places. They are dirty, crowded, even dangerous places, but they are full to overflowing with beautiful people.

Questions for Groups or Individuals

1. Discuss the models of urban ministry described in the chapter. How does each demonstrate hope for the city?

2. If you live in or near a city, how many different cultural groups are you aware of? Where do they live? Are there ethnic churches?

3. What are the implications of the cultural diversity of urban areas?

4. Read Philippians 2:5-11. What does incarnational ministry mean to you?

5. What would imitating Christ's model of ministry mean in the context of urban ministry?

6. How does your definition of "missionary" change in light of the rapid urbanization of the world?

7. How might you change your plans for preparation for ministry to accommodate this reality?

For Further Study

Urbana Tapes

Plenary Session #4, Glandion Carney.

God Is Building a City, 2100 Productions.

Audio #7189, "Hope for the Cities," Glandion Carney.

Bible Studies

Carney, Glandion. *Urbanization.* Global Issues Bible Studies. Downers Grove, Ill.: InterVarsity Press, 1990.

Webb, Jana L. *Economic Justice.* Global Issues Bible Studies. Downers Grove, Ill.: InterVarsity Press, 1990.

Books

Bakke, Ray. *The Urban Christian.* Downers Grove, Ill.: Inter-Varsity Press, 1987. A focus on ministry in North American cities.

Grigg, Viv. *Companion to the Poor.* Monrovia, Calif.: MARC, 1990. Viv's account of planting a church in a Manila squatter community.

LaPierre, Dominique. *The City of Joy.* New York, N.Y.: Warner, 1985. A moving account of the life of Calcutta's slum dwellers.

8

Students Offering Hope

Paul Tokunaga remembers the day he began to fall in love with his campus. It was a sunny spring day, nearly twenty years ago, and Paul was a sophomore at Cal Poly in San Luis Obispo. He was relaxing in the upper deck of the student union courtyard, while down below students gathered for a political demonstration.

"As I watched," Paul recalls, "it became crystal clear to me: these are sheep, lots of them, without a shepherd. They need the Lord." Paul watched them, and imagined the pain and hurt represented in those hundreds of lives. "The more I thought about being a student without Jesus Christ, the more I wept. I was crying for the soul of the campus." The compassion he felt motivated a tentative prayer: "Lord, will you love the campus ... through me?"

Paul was part of the InterVarsity fellowship on campus, a group of 60 to 70 Christians who were not quite a force to be reckoned with on campus. He joined with a few other underclassmen, all of them naive enough to believe they could make a bigger impact on the lives of students around them. Their vision took shape. "We wanted more than anything else, to see Cal Poly—the whole campus—wrestle with the greatness of Jesus Christ."

They started small, trying to be good roommates, studying with classmates and sharing about Christ when it was appropriate. They joined campus organizations—the newspaper, arts groups and ethnic clubs as well as sororities and fraternities—serving others and integrating their faith with campus life.

Several ran for student government offices on a Christ-centered platform. They lost the election, but one of Paul's opponents for student-body president approached him one day and said, "I thought I was a Christian, but I've watched your party's campaign. You love each other, and you love us, your enemies. How can I know this Jesus you're talking about?"

This new student-body president hired Paul as his public relations director, and one of Paul's unofficial duties was to disciple him. "We met every Monday through Friday, from 7:30 to 8:00 a.m. in his office, for Bible study and prayer."

The commitment to love the campus was costly too. Paul wrote the college president a letter early in his sophomore year. He introduced himself as a Christian, and explained that he was committed to nonviolence and peace on campus. Those were tense and often violent days on American campuses, and Paul offered to help in any way he could. Much to his surprise, the college president called him one Sunday afternoon in April.

It was a few days before a major campus rally. Radicals had promised to shut down the country on May Day 1971. The president said, "Paul—this rally on Thursday—I'm scared. What do you think I should do?"

The president asked for Christians to help protect the campus, rather than calling in the National Guard. Paul and his friends knew they were putting themselves in physical danger, but as he explains, "By that point we were victims of love. We loved Cal Poly too much to turn our backs on our campus. No longer was the campus our adversary. It had become our friend.

"That Thursday came. The auditorium was jammed with over 1,000 students. There I was, aisle C, third row, leaning forward, ready to leap up and grab the mike as soon as the radical leader yelled, 'Let's tear apart the administration building!'

"I prayed, 'Oh Lord, pudgy Japanese-American guys with acne—we don't usually do this kind of thing. But if you're in it, I'm in it.'

"Our biggest guys were ready to block the exits. More importantly, over 1,000 fellow Christian students throughout California were praying for us. By the end of the meeting, Tom Hayden, generally a rousing speaker, had literally put some students to sleep. Our God reigned."

Paul's prayer that God would love the campus through him was being answered. By the time Paul graduated, thousands of students had been challenged to consider Christ through the life and witness of Christian students. And the legacy of their love for the campus continues. The InterVarsity chapter thrives today, with more than 400 students who are continuing to confront their fellow students with the love of Jesus. Paul has gone on to minister to other students, and now serves as the regional director for InterVarsity in the southeastern United States.

What Students Can Do

Student ministry is an important key to world evangelization. Not only are college and university students around the world an open and accessible mission field, they are also a powerful missionary force in their own right. Just as Paul Tokunaga and his friends prayed and dreamed of ways of engaging their campus with the gospel, so students around the world today are pioneering evangelistic outreaches to their campuses and nations. Ada Lum has served for 36 years with the International Fellowship of Evangelical Students (IFES), a fellowship of some 130 indigenous student movements, including InterVarsity in the United States and Canada. Originally she planned to work with students in her home state of Hawaii for three years, then return to serve in a local church. Then she began to see the impact of students like Irving.

Irving was an enthusiastic, bright student who had lots of ideas for improving his church. He met some Christians on the campus of the University of Hawaii and became a Christian through them.

"He realized that he had been having good ideas about how to change the church around without even knowing God," says Ada. "He went back to his church and began to talk with the pastor about having group Bible studies. Within a year that church was really turned around because one student learned to use his gifts for the kingdom of God."

Ada's opinion of student work had been turned around too: "I saw student work as a wonderful strategy. I saw the students as God's agents to bring new life, new hope for the languishing churches."

Students Founding Churches

Sometimes student groups are the founding cores of new churches. In December 1989 more than 800 people gathered for a conference called "Chinese Mission 89." They represented many of the 900 ethnic Chinese churches in the United States and Canada.

According to Dr. Gail Law, who now teaches at the China School of Theology in Hong Kong, most Chinese churches in North America began as campus Bible-study groups. Student fellowships have birthed churches and a growing missionary involvement.

One of Ada Lum's colleagues, Gwen Wong, travelled to the Philippines in the 1950s to begin a student ministry there. She found a group of six or seven students who were meeting for prayer and Bible study, and she began to meet with them and help them. "She encouraged them to take the initiative and responsibility for campus evangelism," Ada explains.

After about six years, Gwen felt it was time to move on. Some missionaries told her that the budding student movement would collapse without her supervision. "Gwen, you are being idealistic to think you can leave the student work so soon," they said. "We've been here for 10, 15, 20 years. The Filipinos still need us. They still need you, Gwen."

Gwen left, but the students thrived more than 30 years later, the Philippine InterVarsity movement is one of the strongest in Asia. They have sent missionaries from Manila to other parts of the country, as well as other countries throughout the world.

Ada visited the Philippines several years after Gwen left. One of the missionaries who had criticized Gwen for leaving told her, "The Philippine IVCF has made a world of difference in our churches and in our nation."

Many other successful student movements have begun as pioneering efforts with just a handful of committed students who want to see God make a difference in their campuses, churches and country.

Chile was one of those movements when Ada visited there a number of years ago to train students to lead evangelistic Bible studies. She stayed with Josue and Erica, a couple who were sacrificially giving of themselves to help the new student ministry.

Ada describes her first evening with them. "It was the dead of winter, and it was cold, but I didn't tell them I felt cold. We had a very simple meal of rice and egg. Afterward, I learned that was their last egg and their last cup of rice. It happened that someone had given me an envelope to give to them, and later Josue said there was enough money in it to feed us while I was there. They didn't talk about sacrifice; they just sacrificed for Jesus' sake."

Last summer, Ada attended a conference of the Nigerian student ministry, NIFES. It is the largest IFES movement, with 40,000 members, and eighteen staff members who cover 20 to 25 campuses each.

Femi Adeleye, general secretary of NIFES, sees the movement as more than a way of reaching students with the gospel. In a country where there are periodic political upheavals, economic dislocations following changes in the oil market, religious riots between Muslims and Christians, and tribal jealousies of all sorts, students can make a difference. As Femi expressed it to Ada, "NIFES is one of the very few inter-tribal organizations— even among Christians. They are our great hope for Nigeria."

Students in Mission

Students represent not only a future hope for their nations and the world. They are a powerful force for evangelism and mission now. Students and recent graduates have access to most countries of the world through academic exchanges and other study programs. Christianity started as a young people's movement— after all, Jesus was only 33 when he died—and young men and women have been on the frontlines since Paul left Timothy to supervise the church in Ephesus.

Victor Santana, a student at Trinity Evangelical Divinity School, struggled with doubts about whether God could use him as part of an InterVarsity summer mission team in the Soviet Union. As he got to know Soviet students whose world view was steeped in atheism, he wondered how he would communicate his faith to them. "If they don't see God, it's hard for them to believe," he says. "This really hurt me, and it brought me many doubts." Still, he waited for God to open a door.

One day, he walked into a room where some Soviet and American students were gathered. One of the Soviet women caught his attention. "I had compassion for her, because I saw that she was really hurting inside. It was as if she had a lot of emptiness inside and was searching for the answer, for the truth." He started a conversation with her and began to present the gospel to her. Midway through he noticed she was crying. He asked her what was wrong.

"Victor, I don't know why, but while you were speaking I suddenly felt this peace and joy that I have never felt before. What is it?"

And Victor explained that it was the Lord knocking at the door of her heart. She received Christ that day, and Victor was reminded that God is the one who converts people, and he works through people, even those who feel inadequate.

George Otis, Jr., went to the mission field right out of high school, serving with Youth With A Mission for seven years in Europe. He returned to the United States at the age of 25 and faced a crisis. "All of my friends and peers were now graduated from college, moving on in their careers, almost every one of them was married. I was single, I had no college education, no career. I suddenly felt these pangs of doubt—was what I had done with my life legitimate?"

George struggled with the doubt and turmoil he felt about his decision to serve the Lord until one day he poured out his heart to God.

The response surprised him. "It was as if the Lord flipped a switch on a projector and the last seven years of my life came before my eyes again. I saw myself witnessing to people. I saw myself leading people to the Lord, praying for people, mobilizing people for mission—in graphic detail that under normal circumstances I would not have recalled. Then just as quickly as it had begun the projector went off. The Lord said to me, 'Your concern is that you don't have a relationship, a college education, a career. You can still have any and all of those things, but you can never give me your youth again.' "

The energy and idealism of young people whose lives are gripped by the love of Christ and love for people is a force that will make a difference in this world.

Questions for Groups or Individuals

1. Discuss Paul Tokunaga's account of outreach at Cal Poly. (What was their strategy?)

2. How might you apply a similar strategy to your campus or workplace?

3. What are some of the characteristics of student movements around the world?

4. What kind of impact can they make in their own countries?

5. Do you think of Christianity as a youth movement? Why or why not?

For Further Study
Urbana Tapes

Plenary Session Video #5, *Friends,* Paul Tokunaga.

Plenary Session Video #7, *Students in World Mission,* Ada Lum.

Audio #7190, "Hope for the Student World," Paul Tokunaga.

Audio #7191, "Hope for Students of the World," Ada Lum.

Bible Studies

Lau, Lawson. *Declare His Glory Among the Nations.* Champaign, Ill.: Leadership Publications.

Books

Bieler, Stacy, and Dick Andrews. *China at Your Doorstep.* Downers Grove, Ill.: InterVarsity Press. A guide to ministry with Chinese international students.

9

Hope and Holiness

The sin and suffering of the world demonstrate its need for a Savior and Lord. They also point to the need for messengers of the gospel who will themselves be good news. One doesn't have to look far to find people whose lack of personal integrity and holiness has made a more lasting impression on the world than their testimony for Christ.

Philemon Choi, who was born in mainland China and raised in Hong Kong, reflects on the slow progress of the gospel in some parts of China during the missionary era—"not because of the offensiveness of the gospel, but because of the unholy living of some of the messengers."

Heavenly Minded

In Colossians 3, Paul turns to the problems of holy living, urging Christians to live the kind of life that will not prove a barrier to the faith of others. It's a battle fought primarily in the mind: "Set your minds on things above, not on earthly things."

Some accuse Christians of being so focused on heavenly reality that they are of no earthly good. Leonard Ravenhill countered that argument with his comment, "A lot of Christians are so earthly minded that they are of no heavenly use."[1]

The mission of the church, the work of Christ are not exercises in human ingenuity or dedication. As good as all our works of service and sacrifice might be by themselves, they are never going to change the world. "For our struggle is not against flesh and blood, but against the rulers, against the authorities, against the powers of this dark world and against the spiritual forces of evil in the heavenly realms" (Eph 6:12).

Paul offers two lists of attitudes and behaviors that Christians should get rid of. The first deals essentially with greed. "Put to death, therefore, whatever belongs to your earthly nature: sexual immorality, impurity, lust, evil desires, and greed, which is idolatry" (Col 3:5).

These things relate to our motivations and desires in relation to things or people, and our attempt to let our God-given desires take the place of God in our lives. Paul equates greed with idolatry. Our attempt to live a holy life is in jeopardy whenever we put our trust in something other than God—whether it is sexual pleasure, power or money—and hope that it will fulfill our deepest needs. They exert their addicting power, and we become their victims. The second list has to do with emotions and words. "But now you must rid yourselves of all such things

as these: anger, rage, malice, slander and filthy language from
your lips. Do not lie to each other" (Col 3:8).

Anger is the root of these sins, and anger is usually a symptom of damaged emotions or broken relationships. Henri Nouwen has pointed out, "When my sense of self depends on what
others say of me, anger is quite a natural reaction to a critical
word."[2] Hurt puts us on the defensive and works against our
capacity for healthy relationships.

Giving up Anger

Philemon Choi tells of his struggle with anger as a young man
called to ministry. As the eldest son in a Chinese family, he
knew his father expected him to be successful in his medical
career, but he wanted his father's approval for his decision to
go into ministry. "I approached him, and shared with him what
the Lord wanted me to do. Hesitantly, trembling, I disclosed it
bit by bit. Finally, I told him exactly what I was going to do.
He gave me a three-hour lecture."

Philemon was devastated and angry, but his culture had
taught him to suppress his anger, that it wasn't appropriate to
be angry with his father. But the anger didn't go away. "Damaged emotions don't just disappear," Philemon explains. "Sometimes they turn into words, and in my ungodly moment, I had
some unkind words for my father."

He struggled with the anger and depression until one of his
seminary classes touched on the issue of emotions. The professor invited him to role-play his anger toward his father, then
startled him with the suggestion that he should reverse roles
and play his father. "Then I discovered my father was wounded.
I thought I was the only one wounded, but he was wounded by
my attitude."

Philemon confessed his anger and discovered that ridding his life of anger and greed makes room for the traits God desires. "When Jesus Christ helped me to nail my anger and grief to the cross, he came in and replaced it with something else, with compassion, kindness, humility, gentleness."

These are the things Colossians tells us to clothe ourselves with. They are the marks of a renewed life. Love and humility and compassion are the salve for the world's wounds.

Ministering Out of Humility

Not long ago, Philemon was invited to minister in Hong Kong's Stanley prison, where those convicted of murder and sentenced to either death or life imprisonment serve. He trembled a bit as he entered the hall where 100 prisoners had gathered. "But the moment I stood up there, I could sense love in that room. I was surprised." Some of the men responded to his message and wanted to accept Christ.

Later, Philemon discovered that he wasn't the first one to share the love of Christ with these prisoners. There was a German woman who had been visiting the prison every day for eight years. The men called her "Mum." She reached out to them in humility and compassion, befriending them, serving them by bringing little things like guitar strings that they couldn't get otherwise.

Philemon met the woman one day, "She said she would be in Hong Kong for a long time because she has all her sons in that prison." Most Hong Kong residents are desperate to leave the country before 1997 when the Chinese government will take control. Thus, Philemon was impressed with this woman's willingness to stay beyond her retirement because of her dedicated love for those prisoners.

Paul sums up his appeal for holy living in Colossians by returning to the issue of our minds. "Let the word of Christ dwell in you richly."

The battle to live holy lives worthy of the gospel calling is not won in a day. It's a constant call to remember who we are in Christ—children of a holy God, sinners bought with a price—and to live that way. In a world that's characterized by war and strife, where the specter of AIDS threatens hundreds of millions, the witness of a holy life is vital.

Questions for Groups or Individuals

1. Read Colossians 3. What does it mean to you to "set your minds on things above" in the context of a concern for mission?

2. Look at Paul's list of sinful attitudes and behaviors (vv. 5-9). How do these things interfere with living out a witness for Jesus?

3. Look at the positive attitudes Paul outlines in verses 12-14. Do you think these will really "work" in the context of a world that might be hostile to our message?

4. Are there relationships in your life where you struggle with anger? How could seeing the situation from the other person's point of view help you resolve conflicts?

For Further Study

Urbana Tapes

Plenary Session Video #6, Philemon Choi.

Audio #7187, "Colossians 3: Spiritual Warfare and Holiness," Philemon Choi.

10

Bringing Racial Reconciliation

C aesar Molebatsi was riding his bike home on Christmas Eve 1964 when he was hit from behind by a car. He lay on the pavement, with his right leg fractured in three places, a 13-inch wound down his side, two of his fingers almost severed and his head injured. The driver of the car, a man with his family on their way out of town for vacation, checked to see that the teenager he had hit was alive, then threw an old blanket over him and drove off.

Eventually, Caesar was picked up by a police van and driven to a hospital. There the doctors agreed his condition was serious but they couldn't admit him. It was a White hospital. They couldn't put a Black teen in a "White" bed. The police drove

Caesar to another hospital twenty miles away, where he was operated on.

Two weeks later, though, the doctors discovered gangrene in his injured leg. Caesar's right leg was amputated.

"And with that leg went all desire to live," recalls Caesar. "I was broken, I was destroyed. For three months I sat in that hospital thinking about my body that lay skewered across the tarmac on the 24th of December. And I realized then that there is only one course for me, when I leave this place I must do something about that White man. That's where I was, and that's where the gospel found me."

Caesar grew up in Soweto, profoundly influenced by the apartheid system that institutionalized racism in South Africa. In 1954 the government decided to take Black schools out of the control of churches and mission agencies in order to ensure a substandard level of education for Blacks. Caesar's father, a school teacher, felt betrayed by the church because it didn't protest strongly enough. Besides, he didn't see much difference in the lives of people who went to church compared to those who didn't.

So when Caesar was a young boy, his father decided that the family would no longer go to church. Caesar's view of God was shaped by his father's attitudes. "I came to believe that God had taken the phone off the hook as far as our cries as Black people was concerned."

Love Your Enemy

Thus, Caesar's attitude toward God was indifference, while the accident which cost him his right leg convinced him that White people could only be viewed as the enemy.

Both of those beliefs would be shaken to the core by two men he met at a Christian outreach called Youth Alive. "That's where for the first time I saw a Black person and a White person in one room, not at war." An American missionary named Alan Lutz and a Black youth minister named Jerry Nkose demonstrated the possibility of reconciliation between races as they shared the gospel with Caesar.

"I struggled for three months to try and understand what it means to accept Christ," says Caesar. "The one thing that held me back was I had this sneaky feeling that if I became a Christian, God was going to do something about my feelings about Whites, and I wasn't too sure I was ready to give that up. Finally, on a Sunday afternoon in April 1967, I stood on a busy street and said, 'Lord, if you're real and if your love is real, let it be real to me.'

"The first thing that happened when I went back for counseling was a simple verse read to me by those who had struggled with me for three months to show me the way to the cross. I thought it was cruel at the time, but they told me the Bible says you must love your enemy. Nobody told me that I must read the Bible, but as soon as they told me that there is a verse like that, I had to search through the entire Scripture to make sure that's what God would say because I didn't believe he could. And to my horror—and let me tell you at that time it was a horror—the Bible does say that."

Caesar's struggle with racism didn't end that day. For some time he found it hard to believe that White people could have the same life-transforming relationship to God that he had found. He argued with Alan Lutz and eventually the witness of Lutz and Nkose working in partnership helped him to realize "that there is truth in the fact that the Gospel of Jesus Christ not only reconciled us with God, but it also reconciles us with one another."

Caesar was preaching the gospel one day on a university campus. "A young White man named Jeremy came up and said, 'I want to give my life to Christ. Help me to grow in my spiritual life.' I said okay. I thought it was an easy task—teach him how to read the Bible, pray and give and join the church. Then he was presented with his military service papers. He knew no other person to go to except me, to say, 'Should I join the military?'—knowing that it is used by the South African government to oppress Blacks.

"For the first time in my life I was forced to look at a White person for who he really was. And so over a few months I had to relate to Jeremy who was coming to my home with a crewcut. And Black people were asking, 'What are you doing with these army types?' I had to say, 'He's my brother.' " Caesar is thankful to God that he was given the grace to hold onto Jeremy because that stance is being vindicated by those who are committed to a nonviolent, non-racial future for South Africa.

Multi-Racial Witness

Stacey Chapman discovered the potential there is in a united multi-racial witness. Stacey was part of a very diverse team of InterVarsity students in the Soviet Union in 1990. As she met and travelled with team members who were White, Asian and Hispanic, Stacey began to deal with the fact that all her friends were Black.

"I'd always thought that Whites have a problem getting along with Blacks. Then, when I met this group, I thought, 'How am I going to relate to these people?' "

Before they even arrived in the Soviet Union, they were dealing with issues of racial reconciliation. Stacey describes their experiences as hearing God saying, "I'm going to unveil racism. I'm going to give you an opportunity to know that I really love these different races, and I have brought this group of students together for one purpose." As beneficial as this process was for the thirty team members, the impact on the people they were ministering to was just as great.

They met a young man who spoke Spanish, but not English. The Hispanic team members were able to minister to him, and he became a Christian. "I saw how much you loved each other and worked together, and I knew that the God you served was real," he testified.

In another situation, the team members found themselves the focus of attention at an impromptu press conference in a small town in the Ukraine. One of the questioners pointed out that in Soviet society the only time people of various ethnic and racial backgrounds are together is in the army. He noted that these Americans seemed to enjoy being with one another, and asked, "Don't you have racial prejudice in the United States?"

Stacey stood up and said, "I grew up in the projects of Atlanta. I grew up with the feeling that Blacks are inferior to Whites. Yes, there's racial prejudice in America. And if you see something different in us, it's because we love God. We know who God is, and God is no respecter of persons."

A Heritage of Distrust

Unfortunately, the history of the church and its missionary efforts more often testifies to the disunity and racial separation of believers. Squabbles between Greek- and Aramaic-speaking believers threatened to distract the apostles from their ministry of preaching and teaching in the first years of the church. Not long afterward, Peter argued with God about whether the gospel could possibly apply to the Gentiles.

Even dedicating your life to serving Christ crossculturally does not exempt a person from racial pride, as Ada Lum discovered. In one Asian country where she spent a few years, she was invited to teach at a large student conference. She remembers being embarrassed by the complimentary introduction, until the group's director said, "But we have to pray for Sister Ada the way we pray for all the missionaries. In our culture we know that the two proudest people in the world are the Americans and the Chinese. And Sister Ada is an American and a Chinese. So we have to pray doubly hard for her."

"I was so furious," recalls Ada. But later, "I realized he was right. I did have race prejudice. I thought I loved them, but my love was on the outside. I knew the right things to say, I knew the humble things to say, but these wise, intuitive brothers and sisters knew that in my heart I felt superior to them, more so than the average missionary, because of the double dose of pride. That was one of the most cleansing experiences I ever had on the field."

Many Western missionaries are dedicated to training and helping national leadership, and some even work under the leadership of national Christians. However, the historical associations of mission efforts with political and cultural imperialism lingers in the present church situation in many parts of the world.

A Quechua pastor attending Urbana 90 realized that churches in his area were not growing because of racial tensions between North American missionaries and national church leaders. Misunderstandings and offenses had kept them from working together in harmony, and the pastor was determined to go home and be reconciled with his White brothers and sisters.

The reality of today's church worldwide is that the majority of Christians live outside of the West and are people of color. The composition of the world mission force will soon be more non-Western than Western as well. Yet the stereotype of a missionary as a White, Western, affluent person persists, and no doubt keeps some people from responding to God's call in their lives.

An Asian-American student attending Urbana 90 realized that he was growing increasingly uncomfortable seeing Asian and Asian-American presenters on the platform. "A lot of my experience of intimacy with God has been through Caucasian people, and at the same time a lot of neglect and persecution has come at the hands of my Asian family and friends," he said, explaining that he realized his discomfort was rooted in this experience. "I did not believe that God loved Asians. I think God is showing me through these role models that God loves Asians and Asians do love God."

What the Bible Says

Isaac Canales, pastor of a multi-ethnic church in Los Angeles, looks to the long biblical tradition of what he calls "a theology of welcome."[1] The Lord instructed his people from the beginning to accept foreigners who lived among them: "For the LORD your God is God of gods ... who shows no partiality and accepts no bribes. He defends the cause of the fatherless and the widow, and loves the alien, giving him food and clothing. And you are to love those who are aliens, for you yourselves were aliens in Egypt" (Deut 10:17-19).

This welcome was extended and fulfilled in Jesus' refusal to let Jewish ceremonial law isolate him from people who were the aliens of his day—the tax collectors and sinners, as well as

Samaritans and Gentiles. And the value and importance of each human culture is finally affirmed in the book of Revelation's picture: "After this I looked and there before me was a great multitude that no one could count, from every nation, tribe, people and language, standing before the throne and in front of the Lamb" (Rev 7:9).

A Model of Reconciliation

Glen Kehrein and Raleigh Washington are trying to work out a ministry based on racial reconciliation in Chicago's inner city. Glen directs Circle Urban Ministries, and Raleigh pastors the Rock of our Salvation Evangelical Free Church, which consists of about 70 per cent Black and 30 per cent White members.

"The bigger picture of Christianity is reconciliation," says Glen. "We were alienated from God because of sin; the work of Christ is the work of reconciliation. Racial reconciliation is an application of that bigger picture. The biggest inconsistency we live as Christians is that we preach, 'They'll know we are Christians by our love,' but we live a gospel that creates the most segregated hour of the week at 11:00 Sunday morning."

"The hardest thing for me to accept when I first started ministering in the city was that Black people saw me as a racist," says Glen. He realized that Whites tend to think of racism as something that happened in previous generations or another part of the country, whereas to Blacks "racism is any expression of prejudice, any indication that you don't treat me like a human being or you qualify me by the color of my skin. They see that all around."

Glen and Raleigh discovered that ignoring racial differences did not mean that reconciliation was taking place. "We start from the basis that we understand that Black folks and White folks are not naturally going to get along together. You've got to find out why they don't so there can be reconciliation," explains Raleigh.

Glen recognizes racial reconciliation as one of the keys to successful urban ministry. "If we're not willing to open these areas in ourselves, we find ourselves doing things for people. If we are willing, it's like a burn wound. You don't just bandage it. You need to expose it, put medicine on it, rebandage it. You have to do that over and over, keep taking off the dead skin. That helps the healing process. It comes down to two people being able to work it out."

Glen and Raleigh realized early in their partnership that the relationship between Circle Ministries and Rock Church would mirror the strength or weakness of their relationship. They've also been intentional about encouraging those involved in their ministries to do the work of reconciliation.

When one of Raleigh's church members tells him about a problem with a member of the other race, he urges them to deal with it face-to-face. "I'd say, you need to talk to that White brother or sister about that. I'll tell you what, you have 24 hours. If you don't talk to them, then I'll meet with both of you and get that issue resolved. The tendency is to hear it and empathize with it, and all of a sudden you're building a chasm in racial relations."

Building Unity

Racial reconciliation is an important agenda for churches and missions to pursue, but even more it is a work of grace needed by a world torn apart by racial and ethnic strife. The daily newspaper is full of evidence of racism's destructiveness. Azerbaijanis stand against Armenians. Palestinians are in conflict with Israelis. There are riots in India over concessions given to the untouchables. Amazon tribes are being pushed to the edge of extinction by miners and farmers. Sometimes these battles are fought in terms of religion or culture or economics, but racism or ethnic pride is usually just below the surface.

As prevalent as these conflicts are in our world, South Africa remains the most graphic illustration of racism's evils. But in the struggles of people like Caesar Molebatsi, it may yet offer the most powerful signs of hope for reconciliation. During the past 25 or so years, the Black church in South Africa has played a key role in the effort to create a just, non-racial society in South Africa.

In 1988, Caesar told a North American audience that it was "five minutes past midnight" in his country—the tide was turning toward genuine change. In the past two years, some of apartheid's legal structure has been repealed and Black leaders like Nelson Mandela have been released from prison, but in the midst of these promising signs, 1990 proved a year of horrible violence between rival Black factions. "One hopes," says Caesar, "that what we are seeing is the dark hour before the dawn."

It is a dangerous time to be involved in the struggle for racial justice and reconciliation in South Africa, yet it is also a time of great hope. Caesar points to changing attitudes on local levels, such as some of the White suburbs of Johannesburg near Soweto that have decided to open their school systems to other races rather than seeing schools closed for lack of students.

"Integration and a desire to see all races together, even though it is more difficult than it would be in the United States, is nevertheless something that is much more desired by churches in South Africa." Obstacles include the sheer distances that separate Black and White communities, where

Blacks might have to travel twenty miles—without their own cars—in order to attend church with other races.

Caesar's own painful experience of being liberated from racist attitudes may eventually help others—Black and White—to let go of the fears and hatred that have kept Blacks and Whites apart in South Africa for hundreds of years. "I believe it is going to take Black leaders who have worked through issues of racism themselves to be able to free some of the White people who would like to be freed from the shackles of racism but don't know what to do. I am able to say to a lot of Whites, 'If you think you hated Blacks, you don't know how I hated you. But you want to know how I overcame it? This is how. If you've got problems with Blacks, there's hope for you.'"

The hope demonstrated by a person who has been set free from racism's bondage is truly good news to a world suffering the consequences of racial strife. "To be reconciled racially," says Caesar, "is the way that this world will be made to sit up and listen."

Questions for Groups or Individuals

1. Where do you see evidence of racism? (in your community? church? fellowship? family?)

2. How does racism affect you?

How do you respond to it?

3. Consider the multi-ethnic mission teams described in the chapter. Why is it important for Christians to present a united witness in our world?

4. How can you implement a "theology of welcome"? (Are there Christians around you of other racial or ethnic groups that you can connect with? Where would you begin?)

5. Do you agree with Caesar Molebatsi that racial reconcil-

iation "is the way that this world will be made to sit up and listen"? Why or why not?

For Further Study
Urbana Tapes
Plenary Session Video #6, Caesar Molebatsi.
Audio #7195, "Multi-Ethnic Teams in Mission," Virgil Lee Amos.
Audio #7190, "Hope for Racial Reconciliation," Caesar Mole-batsi.

Bible Studies
Canales, Isaac. *Multi-Ethnicity*. Global Issues Bible Studies. Downers Grove, Ill: InterVarsity Press, 1990.

Books
Bush, Luis, and Lorry Lutz. *Partnering in Ministry*. Downers Grove, Ill.: InterVarsity Press, 1990. Models of international partnership for world mission.

11
Living
Our Hope

Among the greetings and personal messages at the end of the letter to the Colossians is one that must have been very special to them: "Epaphras, who is one of you and a servant of Christ Jesus, sends greetings. He is always wrestling in prayer for you, that you may stand firm in all the will of God" (Col 4:12).

Epaphras was the founder of the Colossian church (1:7), a native of that city who was now living in Rome during Paul's imprisonment. Paul's description of him sums up the life of people gripped by the hope of Christ—he prays, and he is concerned that they understand and obey the will of God. The two things aren't unrelated.

In a world of escalating physical and spiritual needs, those who want to serve Christ must ask themselves, "What is God's will for me?" "Where does he want me to serve?" According to Isaac Canales, "The most important thing for any Christian who asks these questions is to begin by praying. The will of God is to be found in the context of prayer."

The Role of Prayer

Prayer is a serious matter in Paul's estimation. Not only are his letters full of his prayers for the various churches and individuals he writes to, but he makes a point of reminding the Colossians to pray. "Devote yourselves to prayer, being watchful and thankful. And pray for us, too, that God may open a door for our message" (Col 4:2-3). The word Paul uses to describe Epaphras' prayer for the Colossians is related to the English word *agony*. He agonizes in prayer for them. This is serious work. There's no bland "God bless the Colossians" here.

This kind of prayer demands something of us. Even to know how to intercede effectively for the needs of the world requires an investment on our part, as George Otis, Jr., points out. "We have to be proactive in our Christian walk. We need to choose to expose ourselves to information and relationships that will flesh out our world view and our prayer life. We should not expect God to come and do these things for us. We do it, because we're the ones who have been told to go. When Jesus himself went and saw he had the corresponding emotional reaction, where he was moved with compassion."

George believes it is unrealistic to expect to have much compassion for the lost or motivation to pray without at least being exposed to them. He advocates periodic times of overseas travel in order to develop that compassion and motivation to dedicated prayer—"To say, 'I'm investing in my ministry, in my Christian walk, by exposing myself to the world in 1991.' "

The Power of Personal Prayer

Keren Everett discovered the power of prayer soon after moving with her parents, Al and Sue Graham, into a remote area of the Brazilian jungle, where they were to begin the task of translating the Bible into the Satere language. After five months in the jungle both Al and Sue contracted hepatitis. Within two weeks they were both unable to care for themselves and far too weak to retrace the month of river travel that would take them to the nearest hospital. Finally, Al told the three children, aged seven to nine, that he and their mother were dying. The children would have to find their way out of the village with the Indians' help.

Keren heard her father's words but couldn't accept the frightening reality. She ran out and threw herself on the ground, sobbing. Overwhelmed by the thought of being alone without her parents, Keren's thoughts turned to prayer. But how could she pray? All her life her parents had guided her prayers, in family devotions, at meals, before bed. "As I sat there and thought of praying," Keren recalls, "I knew that I would have to believe that God loved and cared for me, totally apart from Mom and Dad. For the first time I began to pray to God as my true Father."

Keren pleaded for God to save her parents. She had barely finished praying when a friend ran up to her, saying that two strangers had appeared on the river near the village. They were two men she recognized as members of Wycliffe Bible Translators, doing survey work in the area. They took one look at the Grahams and sprang into action, packing supplies and paddling night and day to get the family to the city in four days.

Both Al and Sue recovered, and despite the warnings of doctors they were determined to return to the Satere people. Their 26 years of prayer and service to the Satere has resulted in the completion of the New Testament. There are at least fifteen churches up and down the river, formed as the Satere have read the Scripture in their own language and found hope in Jesus.

Keren returned to the village for the dedication of the Satere New Testament in 1986. Seleh, the girl who had taught her to row a canoe without flipping it, embraced her and told her that she prayed for Keren's family every day. During the service, one of the Satere pastors prayed for at least a dozen indigenous groups in Brazil which still have not received the message of the gospel.

The Power of Corporate Prayer
The centrality and power of prayer was modeled at Urbana 90 by intercessory and prayer ministry teams. The intercessors, a group of thirty dedicated prayer warriors, labored behind the scenes 24 hours a day. They took a group of thirty student interns under their wings and attempted to pass on to them the discipline of intercession.

The prayer ministry team, under the leadership of Rev. Mike Flynn of St. Jude's Episcopal Church in Burbank, California, counselled and prayed with students who were dealing with brokenness and family dysfunctionality, including more than 2,000 who came forward after the plenary session on that topic. "I prayed for someone who had been sexually abused, someone with MS and someone else with lupus," said Sharon Stockdale. "Suddenly I saw a woman who was glowing, with tears streaming down her face. She had just received a deep healing and felt great joy."

Mike Flynn was surprised by the depth of needs represented by those who attended an afternoon workshop on sexual healing. "I had to deploy two teams just to hear confessions. Another three or four teams were doing deep one-on-one ministry with people who were incredibly beat up. Any number of incest victims came forward," he recalls. Yet there were amazing transformations experienced that day. "When you're praying for somebody, the Lord can do major, major surgery. Some life-changing things happened."

Mary Anne Voelkel, who led the corporate prayer times for the convention, describes how images from Scripture helped to shape her prayer ministry. "I felt so inadequate for this, but I read about Moses' struggle with inadequacy. When I got to Exodus 17 and the story about the water from the rock, I felt God saying that he wanted to refresh his people."

Mary Anne began reading various books on prayer, searching for models of corporate prayer. "I thought about David and Goliath—how David tried to wear other people's armor, but it didn't fit. I knew how to use prayer 'stones'—things that had been meaningful to me in prayer, like loving God, being silent and listening to God, interceding, spiritual warfare, and praying with other people." Each of those elements was woven into the times of prayer.

Ultimately it is hope and faith that keep us at the hard work of agonizing prayer. "The basis of hope, and certainly of faith, is entering into what God says he is going to do," says Mary Anne. Biblical promises gave her and other members of the prayer team confidence that "the Lord himself was going to heal, refresh, and pour out his Spirit. I like to pray the Scriptures, and certain ones were quickened to me that gave real hope."

Answered Prayers

Perhaps the greatest sustainer of confident prayer is seeing answers. The night before the convention started some of the video projectors were left out in subzero weather, which cracked the lenses. A half-million dollars' worth of equipment was damaged, but through prayer and some urgent calls, replacements were found within hours. "Visible answers give faith for the invisible ones—the things that are harder to see," says Mary Anne.

Students testified to some of those less visible answers as they shared how God had worked in their hearts. "The Lord has given me a real hope and heart for the world, and specifically urban missions," said one student. A medical student explained she had come to Urbana "feeling burned out about trying to reach people on her campus." During the convention, she had a chance to share her renewed vision with a fellow student. "We are committed to praying that Jesus would take our campus over for himself," she said.

A deaf collegian was convicted that she needed to be reconciled with hearing people. "So I'm giving up my anger and bitterness, and I want to help other deaf people to reconcile with hearing people," she said.

Serving Obediently

As important as prayer is, faithful obedience is just as critical to those who want to serve Christ. Just as Paul encouraged the Colossians to intercede for him and his ministry, he urged them to be faithful to God's call in their lives too. "Be wise in the way you act toward outsiders; make the most of every opportunity. Let your conversation be always full of grace, seasoned with salt, so that you may know how to answer everyone" (Col 4:5-

6). He asked them to pray for an open door for the message and effective proclamation. He clearly anticipates that they will find open doors—opportunities or *kairos* moments—when they can share the good news with those around them.

Going through the open door might look different depending on the circumstances, but the person transformed by "Christ in you, the hope of glory" must be ready to articulate that hope.

Mark Ritchie tells of his father's ministry as a tentmaker in Afghanistan, a country where "it was strictly forbidden even to mention the name of Christ, even to leave your Bible out where someone could see it." Dwight Ritchie worked as an engineer there, returned to the States for a number of years, and then went back to help build a hospital in a remote city. He was killed in a car accident.

Mark tells of the pilot who flew the body back to the capital, a man who remembered Dwight from his own school days. "They asked him, 'What did this foreigner teach you?' He said, 'He taught me surveying. He taught me, "when I survey the wondrous cross." ' "

Though he was restricted in the words he could say, Dwight obviously walked wisely among the people of Afghanistan.

Depending on God

What kind of people can God use to do his work in the world? A look at some of the people Paul mentions at the end of his letter to the Colossians gives a hint.

Onesimus, who along with Tychicus was going to deliver the letter, was a runaway slave before he became a Christian. Paul had interceded on his behalf with his master, Philemon, to win his freedom. Paul also included a specific reminder that the Colossians should welcome Mark if he came to see them. Mark's early failure as a missionary had caused a sharp disagreement between Paul and Barnabas, but their partnership in ministry had been restored. These weren't perfect, successful people, but they were faithful to Christ, and God was using them to build his kingdom.

Aristarchus was imprisoned with Paul, possibly they were even chained together, as Isaac Canales suggests: "When they shook hands, the sound of their chains filled the room. In weakness they were able to serve the Lord. God calls us to serve him in weakness because it's only when we are weak that he is strong. Never claim strength, never claim sufficiency. Claim weakness and God will be strength for you wherever you are."

Mike Flynn practices this kind of vulnerability in his healing ministry. "Once you get to the point of saying, 'Come Holy Spirit' all bets are off. You don't know what's going to happen. We think that not knowing is very important because it allows the Holy Spirit to have hands-on control of the gathering." Mike calls this attitude "the immediacy of dependency," a recognition that the powerful, life-transforming work of God doesn't depend on our abilities, but on our willingness to let him work through us. "It's scary. I don't make any bones about how scary it can be. It's uncomfortable. But our discomfort is small price to pay for the effectiveness of God. If we're after his reputation, what difference does it make if we're uncomfortable?"

Mike's church has attracted a number of furloughed missionaries who come to the area to study. Many of them, he reports, come back from the field tired and hurt. It has to do with learning to depend on God, Mike thinks. "We're finding that missionaries who have had a kind of immediacy of dependency and a vulnerability and a functioning relationship with the

Lord in intimacy and dependency don't tend to get as beat up, and they tend to be quite a bit more effective. Missionaries without that come home for a breath of air. A lot of them are brokenhearted, over the difficulties, relationships and mostly over ineffectiveness. They were never initiated in the resources to handle problems, whether they are relationship problems or problems with witch doctors."

Mike reflects on Jesus' last instructions to the disciples before his ascension. He told them to wait in Jerusalem until they received power from the Holy Spirit. Their years of discipleship, witnessing Jesus' healings, teachings and miracles, were not enough to equip them for ministry. "I think the message there is God says, 'It takes my power to do my work. I'm not going to use your power.' "

Prayer reminds us that we are dependent on God—not only for him to reveal his will, but to empower us to carry it out. We are a people transformed by hope, but not hope in ourselves. The world will see the power of God working through us when we demonstrate our dependence on him.

Questions for Groups or Individuals

1. Read Colossians 4. Are you an activist who finds it hard to sit still for prayer or a contemplative who finds it hard to put your faith into action? Explain.

2. What does this chapter say to you about the balance between activism and contemplation?

3. Consider whether your prayer life is characterized by agonizing prayer. How can you deepen your compassion for the people you pray for regularly?

4. What does it mean to you to "walk wisely" and "make the most of every opportunity"?

How do you put these things into practice in your daily life?

5. Look at the characters Paul mentions in his closing remarks. Which of their stories specifically encourages you today?

For Further Study

Urbana Tapes

Plenary Session Video #8, Isaac Canales.

Audio #7187, "Colossians 4: Guidance," Isaac Canales.

Audio #7439, "Spiritual Warfare in Mission," Dr. Jack Voelkel.

Audio #7411, "Spirituality and Prayer," Jim Berney.

Bible Studies

Glasser, Art. *Spiritual Conflict.* Global Issues Bible Studies. Downers Grove, Ill.: InterVarsity Press, 1990.

Books

Carney, Glandion. *Heaven Within These Walls.* Ventura, Calif.: Regal, 1989. An exploration of the "journey inward" of prayer and worship and the "journey outward" of service and ministry.

Hybels, Bill. *Too Busy Not to Pray.* Downers Grove, Ill.: InterVarsity Press, 1988. Insights from a busy pastor who decided to do more than study prayer—he prayed.

12
Moving
Out

P aul Leary was a college junior when he attended Urbana 79. "Only a year before I had asked Jesus to be Lord of my life, as long as he wouldn't send me to Africa," he recalls. By the end of the convention he committed himself to being a witness to those who had never heard of Jesus' love. He also signed up to serve on a summer project in the Central African Republic.

That experience helped shape his vision for serving God overseas. "The people in Africa stole my heart," says Paul. "I returned to the United States convinced that one day I would work with unreached people there." But he wasn't sure how or when he would get there. His parents urged him to find a job in business using his finance major. The InterVarsity staffworker on his campus presented the option of student ministry as a preparation for future mission work. "After five months of waiting on the Lord, it became clear that InterVarsity would be the best option for a couple of years before heading off to Africa."

Those two years stretched out into ten—not because Paul lost sight of his goal, but because of something bigger God was doing. Paul spent those years in campus ministry, developing his ministry skills and imparting them to students. Along the way, he has shared his vision for God's work in the world. More than 100 of his former students are preparing for mission service.

During his campus ministry years, Paul met his future wife, Lynn, a former IVCF staffworker. Paul and Lynn have been called into ministry with a team of four other couples, all of whom share common experiences with InterVarsity and a common vision for mission. "We got together at Easter in 1985 to draw up a covenant that would define our vision for team ministry in Africa," says Paul. "As we talked about what the covenant would include we joked that it felt like talking about marriage. We did not know yet what country, which mission board, but our covenant encapsulated our hopes and dreams about serving God in unreached people groups in Africa."

Today the team members are preparing to work with the Babwisi people of western Uganda. One couple has gone through Wycliffe Bible Translators' linguistic training in order to give the Babwisi the Scriptures in their own language. Two others have completed medical training in preparation for community health evangelism in a region where forty per cent of the children die by the age of three. Another couple has been pastoring rural churches in North Carolina as preparation for training Ugandan pastors. Paul and Lynn will move to Uganda sometime in 1991 to begin preaching the gospel and discipling Ugandan leaders.

Paul Leary is just one of the 140,000 students who have attended an Urbana convention since 1946, many of whom have made commitments to serve the Lord in other cultures as a result of Urbana conventions over the years.

Students have long been a key force in spearheading mission efforts. In the decades just before and after 1900, the Student Volunteer Movement captured the hearts of students across the country with its call to evangelize the world "in our generation." Some 20,000 missionaries fanned out across Asia, Africa and Latin America in response. As the year 2000—understood not as a magical number but as a reminder that the task grows more urgent each day—approaches, there are hopeful signs of a new generation of messengers being raised up to take the good news to those who need to hear it.

Student Mission Efforts

The church in South Korea is an inspiration to many around the world. Several of the largest churches in the world are in Seoul, and Korean missionaries serve all around the world. Korean churches in North America are just as vital. Their desire to see Koreans in this country participate in fulfilling the Great Commission has led to the Korean Mission Council, an unprecedented interdenominational movement.

Early in 1990, a group of young Korean-American leaders met in Los Angeles (home to about 600 of the country's 2,000 Korean churches) to plan ways to mobilize their churches and members for world mission. They were especially concerned with the growing number of young people, mostly second-generation Americans who are more comfortable speaking English than Korean. As they talked and prayed, they set a goal: to recruit and send 1,000 missionaries from their congregations by 2000. They also realized that they would need to see about $25 million per year committed to support that many new workers.

Urbana was their first step, according to Peter Cha, an InterVarsity staffworker in the Chicago area. They wanted to see 1,000 Korean-American students attend the convention, and began to talk to pastors and write articles for Korean-language newspapers. Peter estimates that between 1,200 and 1,500 attended. Around 300 of them indicated that they had made a commitment to serve as career missionaries.

"We don't have a blueprint," Peter says of the efforts to channel these students into opportunities to serve. "We are expectant that God will reveal to us what the next step should be. As a movement, we would like to concentrate on unreached people groups. The students' interests are pretty diverse— mostly South America, Asia and Africa, and some are thinking about the Middle East."

Many of the Korean-American delegates found their understanding of God's work in the world expanding. "Many of them come from a church background that is ethnocentric. God has been doing wonderful things in the Korean-American churches, but they began to see that God's kingdom is bigger than that."

The Mission Field at Home

Meanwhile these students are making an impact on their mission field today—their campuses. Peter Cha has been working with a group of about seventy students at the University of Illinois in Chicago. Like many Korean fellowships, it began with Christian students finding each other and meeting for Bible study and prayer. "They have been highly effective in evangelism," says Peter. "The group is about two-thirds Christian, and we saw four or five students become Christian the last quarter." They have also drawn on affinities with other Asian students and now include a number of Filipino and Chinese students.

Unlike Asian-American students, Native Americans are often an invisible group on college campuses, but they too found Urbana an inspiring and encouraging event. Nearly 200 delegates represented the many North American tribes. According to Huron Claus, director of CHIEF (Christian Hope Indian Eskimo Fellowship), "many students come from Indian churches, whether on the reservations or in cities, where the average membership is twenty to forty people. One young woman from the East Coast told me, 'I never knew there were Native Christians outside my own family.' "

Native American collegians meeting together at Urbana were able to encourage each other in the struggles they face as Native Americans living in two worlds. According to Huron, "In general, there's a real emphasis on passing on our heritage to one another. Our students live in the culture of the past and also learn to live in today's society. On top of that to be a Christian is very difficult. They're asking how can I be a strong Christian and take a stand for my faith and at the same time hold on to the special areas of my culture?" Like Christians of any cultural background, Native American students struggle to affirm the aspects of their culture that reflect kingdom values while discerning those areas that they might need to let go of.

Huron reflects the urgency of this struggle in CHIEF's priority on discipleship training and leadership development for the Christian Native American churches. There are some 51 million Native Americans in the Western hemisphere, representing at least 1,200 tribes. Only about eight per cent are Christian.

"We have had the gospel for over 400 years, the percentage should be higher. Why is it so low?" Huron asks.

It's the same question that a friend from Guatemala asked him recently. Coming from the most-evangelized country in Latin America, where 35 per cent of the indigenous community is Christian, this Guatemalan brother said, "We don't need church planting, our biggest need is in building mature churches." He was asking CHIEF to help develop programs to train leaders.

New Partnerships

But the needs of the Christian Native churches have not stopped some Native Americans from dreaming bigger dreams for the kingdom. In 1990 four Native Americans travelled to Mongolia, retracing—with the help of modern air transportation—the path their ancestors may have taken across the Bering Strait many centuries ago. They discovered some aspects of both cultures that were remarkably similar despite the years of separate development, including the shape of some traditional homes, food and customs of hospitality, and even some words in common between Navajo and Mongolian.

For their part, the Mongolians were eager to get to know the Native Americans, for they too had traditions that told them of ancestors who went to live in North America. After a dinner in the tent of a Mongolian herdsman, Flint Poolaw, a member of the Kiowa tribe, shared his testimony. At least fifteen of the Mongolians said they wanted to follow Jesus.

According to Huron, CHIEF plans to continue to send Native Christians into Mongolia, and, as a result of Urbana, will be cooperating with InterVarsity and Frontiers to send Native American young people to other countries as well.

Making the Commitment

The potential impact of the commitments made by students at Urbana 90 won't be fully felt for years, even decades, but there are reasons to be hopeful. Some 6,000 delegates committed themselves to serving Christ in mission either short-term or long-term, and another 4,000 indicated they are seriously considering the possibility. How many will end up in crosscultural ministry? There is no way of telling, but a survey of delegates who made similar commitments in 1984 showed that four years later 43 per cent had either fulfilled their commitment or were still preparing to go.

By the end of the Urbana 90 convention, delegates were sharing plans to live out a revitalized witness on their campuses or participate in a summer mission project. Two who were able to do something almost immediately were Mary Ruth and Bob Curlee.

The Curlees, whose college-age son Tim also attended Urbana, came as representatives of Fuller Seminary where Bob works in the Development Office. Mary Ruth, in particular, had a long-standing interest in urban ministry and left with a great sense of confirmation of that calling. Bob's response to their renewed interest was simple: "I didn't want to talk about it. I wanted to set a deadline to make a decision." The deadline he suggested was Labor Day, but God's deadline was even sooner.

By March first they were in the process of moving into Hollywood and getting involved with the Hollywood Urban Project. The ministry is an outreach to an enclave of Central American immigrants in South Hollywood that started as a summer program sponsored by Hollywood Presbyterian Church. After a few summers of recreational programs for kids, the church began to sponsor small numbers of young people who lived in the community for an eight-month internship. Nearly all of them have stayed involved in the neighborhood. Mary Ruth Curlee plans to assist the Project with her administrative and editorial skills, as well as being involved with junior high girls who are at high risk of dropping out.

For the Curlees, their move into the city was the latest step in a process that's been going on since they left Oklahoma City in 1982. "The normal aspirations of the American dream were hard to give up, even when you intellectualize that you have given them up," explains Bob. "But I like the idea of being able to travel light." They hadn't been able to afford a house in suburban La Crescenta, so they were able to give notice and move quickly when they found an apartment in Hollywood. The downscaling has been a positive experience. Bob talks excitedly of the furniture they gave away to various mission organizations. There are other adjustments to urban living: "We've been hearing gunshots," says Bob. "We weren't used to that. But we knew it was like that, it's part of the territory."

Most importantly, the Curlees have taken to heart the call to invest their lives in the work of the kingdom, not at some vague time in the future, but right now. Their obedience is being echoed in countless ways, big and small, by many of the more than 19,000 people at Urbana.

Getting Ready

In his challenge to Urbana delegates, Peter Kuzmic pointed to the way Jesus prepared his disciples for their first short-term ministry experience. "When he saw the crowds, he had compassion on them, because they were harassed and helpless, like sheep without a shepherd. Then he said to his disciples, 'The harvest is plentiful but the workers are few. Ask the Lord of the harvest, therefore, to send out workers into his harvest field' " (Mt 9:36-38).

There are two pictures in these verses. The sheep are a picture of human need. "They are distressed, with no guidance, no protection, no food," says Peter. "They are scattered, with no voice of authority and certainty to draw them together and provide direction. What a picture of our world—a world that is spiritually blind, socially corrupt, lost, no sense of direction, no hope."

The second picture is of opportunity. The ripe harvest is waiting for workers to bring it in. More than 500 million people in Europe have never opened a Bible, according to Peter. Yet open doors abound. Not long ago Vaclav Havel, the president of Czechoslovakia, announced that his country needed English teachers from abroad to retrain the 20,000 Russian teachers whose jobs had become obsolete.

Peter concluded by telling a Jewish folk story:

When God was creating the world, four angels came by to watch. The first angel watched for a while and said, "Lord God, you are creating something amazing. Why are you doing this?"

The second angel watched and said, "Lord God, you are creating something out of nothing. How can this be possible?" (We moderns would say that the first angel had a philosophical mind and the second was a scientist.)

The third angel came by and watched. And then he started rubbing his hands, and he said, "Lord God, you are creating something big, wonderful and rich. When you finish it, can I have it?" (Coming from an Eastern European country, I suspect this angel was a capitalist.)

The fourth angel watched for a while, and then became restless and said, "Lord God, you are creating something that has not been there before. I don't want to be just a spectator, a passive observer. Can I help you?"

Harvests do not reap themselves, nor can even the most spiritually open people be expected to put their trust in Jesus if no one has told them the good news. Jesus' invitation to follow him is an invitation to look at the world from his point-of-view. To see the needy sheep and the ripe, golden harvest. And to participate with him in the creation of a new humanity.

Questions for Groups or Individuals

1. How would you characterize your commitment to world mission and your sense of God's direction in your life?

2. What single area of ministry or part of the world would you most like to pursue further, either through more study or by getting involved directly?

3. How do you plan to do this?

4. Who are the people around you who can help nurture your vision and commitment for mission?

5. Who can you share what you have learned about God's work in the world with?

For Further Study

Urbana Tapes
Plenary Session #7, Peter Kuzmic.
Audio #7191, "Call to Commitment," Peter Kuzmic.

Books
Borthwick, Paul. *A Mind for Mission.* Colorado Springs, Colo.: NavPress, 1987. Ten building blocks for growing in your understanding and involvement in mission.

13

A Sustaining Hope

T he Bible says that "hope that is seen is no hope at all"
(Rom 8:24). Sometimes hope is most evident in the most
difficult and apparently hopeless situations, as many on
the frontlines of the kingdom's advance testify.

Over the past seven years, Sri Lanka, a country with only
about two per cent Christians, has been torn by bloody civil war
between the dominant Sinhalese Buddhists and the Tamil Hindu minority. Ajith Fernando, director of Youth for Christ in Sri
Lanka, reports that the most exciting growth in the church is
happening in the part of the country hardest hit by the violence,
where thousands of people have been killed.

"We had always thought of that area as the hardest to reach
in the country, but I went there twice in the last three months

of 1990 to do teaching with the new converts, and it's amazing what is happening. In the aftermath of all the pain—and there is hardly a home where one person hasn't died—the comfort of Jesus, the love of Jesus, the fact that God is a personal God, all of that is real and people are responding to that." A number of former terrorists who have converted are now working with Youth for Christ as staff or volunteers.

Costly Service

The choice to be involved in ministry in these most receptive areas is a costly one. One YFC staff couple in Jaffna have two young children, yet they decided to stay on even after a bomb fell just outside their home. Their evangelistic program on Christmas Day 1990 was attended by 400 young people—a staggering number, says Ajith Fernando, in an area where fifty would have been considered a very good turnout.

For those in youth work, seeing so many young lives destroyed by violence can be a depressing reality. "What has helped me is the vision of the sovereignty of God, that if we are obedient to him in our country, he's going to use our obedience to build his eternal kingdom" says Ajith.

Ajith talks about a decision he and his wife made while they were on sabbatical in the United States a year ago. A radical Communist group was threatening to take over the government, putting Christian organizations like Youth for Christ at risk of very harsh restrictions. "We decided that if this happens, we'd go back right away. The thing we decided was, whatever happens to us, the fact that we stayed will help the future generations. In the heart of all of that is the idea that God is sovereign. If we're doing his will, it doesn't matter what happens to us."

As director of Breakthrough Ministries in Hong Kong, Philemon Choi knows what it is like to decide to stay in a place with an uncertain future for the sake of the kingdom. He describes the mood in Hong Kong in the aftermath of the June 4, 1989 massacre of students in Tiananmen Square. "The whole city went into depression. It was a corporate depression. Six million people at the same time were depressed and disillusioned."

As they reeled under the loss of the hope they had placed in the student democracy movement and looked forward with foreboding to the reversion of Hong Kong's sovereignty to China in 1997, more and more Hong Kong residents looked for a way out. At least 50,000 people have migrated to other countries each year for the past several years, expressing their lack of hope in Hong Kong's future.

The mass migration has affected the church to an even greater extent. The proportion of Christians leaving the country is at least three times that of the general population for several reasons, explains Philemon Choi. The Hong Kong church is largely an upper-middle class movement, and church members are more likely to have the education and resources that make them attractive to receiving countries. With so many Chinese churches in Toronto, Vancouver and other cities booming, Hong Kong pastors are increasingly offered the opportunity to serve them. Meanwhile, those who can't leave—and Breakthrough estimates that ninety per cent of Hong Kong's youth will still be there after 1997—feel powerless and bitter.

Philemon had a choice. He had been educated in Canada and held Canadian citizenship. But he decided to stay in Hong Kong.

Philemon reflected on his travels in China over the past ten to fifteen years. "They are a wounded people. They have learned not to trust anyone, because during the Cultural Revolution even family members betrayed one another. Then I discovered in the midst of that woundedness the church stood out as a lighthouse of hope. Even during the darkest hour, there were Christians who still faithfully did their jobs, instead of turning their anger into bitterness. They stood out, and in the countryside, village after village turned Christian. When the churches reopened in 1978, every church that was open was packed." The fanatical Red Guard had tried to squelch every sign of Christianity, destroying churches and literature, persecuting and scattering believers, but when it was all over there were close to 70 million Christians, where there had been only 700,000 at the end of the Western missionary era.

"I was educated in the West," says Philemon. "Whenever I looked at Marxism, I always looked at it as an outsider, as basically an ideological conflict. But I never tried to look at it from the other side: What does it feel like to be under this kind of system? Can my faith, my religion, my church thrive under this atmosphere? I was taught it doesn't work."

People have begun to urge Philemon to move Breakthrough from Hong Kong. It is a large ministry with a staff of 120 and a lot of valuable high-tech audio-visual equipment. They argue, "Conserve what you have for the kingdom's sake."

"It sounds very attractive," he replies. "But does it make sense? What is the basis of my hope? Breakthrough was called to serve the young people of Hong Kong. Can I leave them with a good conscience and say, 'God bless you, you can trust in God'?

"I look at what God says in Ezekiel 34. In times of crisis the shepherds should not leave. We are called to protect the sheep. But where is the hope and security for those shepherds in times of danger? God says, 'I will be your shepherd, I will protect the sheep.' He is the shepherd of the shepherds. As long as we are faithful to what the Lord wants us to do, the visible form can change, but no one can quench the essence."

The Source of Hope

That essence—the transforming power of Christ in individual lives—is very evident to George Otis, Jr., as he spends time with Christians living in some of the least-evangelized countries on earth. "One of the greatest sources of hope for me comes as I travel and meet with believers in these front-line countries. The substance in the people's lives, the quality of character, the metal that has been proven under fire remind me every time that there is a God. Their faith is not sophisticated, but powerfully simple."

Hope Endures

Hope in Christ gives us new life and propels us into the world to share hope with others. Yet sometimes in the heat of battle we lose sight of it, until the Lord gently restores our hope, as Keren Everett discovered.

Keren and her husband, Dan, have been engaged over the past thirteen years in the task of translating the Scriptures into the language of the Piraha people in Brazil. The periods of time they have spent living in the jungle with the Piraha have been difficult, especially the first stay. Keren's attempts to learn the language were completely frustrated by the custom that Piraha women don't speak to outsiders. But things became scary the night some traders sold the villagers a case of whiskey and told them to kill the American family. "As we were crawling into our hammocks, we heard the Indian men begin to yell threats about killing us," remembers Keren. Having seen the violence of drunken men before, Dan decided to lock the rest of the family in a small storeroom, the only closed room they had. He sat outside with an unloaded rifle across his lap. The Piraha yelled threats and insults, but Dan didn't respond. Finally, they began to fight each other, swinging machetes. When Keren and the three children emerged from the storeroom the next morning, there was blood all over the house. The men were scattered on the ground in front of the house, some sleeping, some still drunk, some badly injured.

Keren's response wasn't very compassionate. "As I looked at them, I said, 'God how can you love them?' The one feeling I had was hate. I wanted to leave and never go back." She had begun to gather up the blood-stained hammocks and linens to wash them in the river when she heard someone approaching. It was the village chief.

The chief called to Keren and Dan, "Please don't leave. We don't want you to leave. We need you. Our heads are sick with whiskey. We don't mean what we said.'" Then he handed Keren a package. She opened it and found five polished jaguar teeth.

"As I looked at those teeth, they began to sparkle," says Keren. "I was reminded of Christ on the cross. He said to me, 'Keren, I loved you in your sin, and I love these people in their sin.' It was as though all at once I saw all of my false hopes come up before me, all of my own attempts to change these people by my power. God reminded me that it was only when I put my hope in his love for me and his love for the peoples of this earth that I would begin to experience the power, the love that only he can give."

Hope that comes from the reality of Christ within us has a

way of shining through in the darkest circumstances, like those precious jaguar teeth sparkling in the sun. Hope comes from the promise Jesus gave his disciples when he sent them out into the world: "And surely I am with you always, to the very end of the age" (Mt 28:20).

Notes

Chapter Two: Lord of the Universe
[1]Gordon Aeschliman, *GlobalTrends* (Downers Grove, Ill.: InterVarsity Press, 1990), pp. 101-105.

Chapter Five: The Creative Access World
[1]Bryan Truman, *Basic Human Needs,* Global Issues Bible Studies (Downers Grove, Ill.: InterVarsity Press, 1990), p. 11.
[2]As quoted by George Otis, Jr.
[3]*Los Angeles Times,* February 12, 1991.
[4]Gordon Aeschliman, *GlobalTrends,* p. 105.

Chapter Six: God's Day for Eastern Europe
[1]Anita and Peter Deyneka, Jr., *A Song in Siberia* (Elgin, Ill.: David C. Cook, 1977), p. 60.
[2]Anita Deyneka, "God in the Gulag," *Christianity Today,* August 9, 1985, p. 30.
[3]*Los Angeles Times,* March 4, 1991.

Chapter Seven: The Challenge of the Cities
[1]"Mexico City: Drying Up," *The Economist,* September 29, 1990.
[2]Glandion Carney, *Urbanization,* Global Issues Bible Studies (Downers Grove, Ill.: InterVarsity Press, 1990), p. 12.
[3]Gordon Aeschliman, *GlobalTrends,* p. 73.
[4]Ray Bakke, *The Urban Christian* (Downers Grove, Ill.: InterVarsity Press, 1987), p. 78.
[5]Kevin Piecuch, "Islam Finds New Home in Western Europe," *Christianity Today,* March 5, 1990.

Chapter Nine: Hope and Holiness
[1]Leonard Ravenhill, *Why Revival Tarries.*
[2]Henri Nouwen, *The Way of the Heart.*

Chapter Ten: Bringing Racial Reconciliation
[1]Isaac Canales, *Multi-Ethnicity,* Global Issues Bible Study (Downers Grove, Ill.: InterVarsity Press, 1990), pp. 11-14.

Resources

The following materials were produced in conjunction with Urbana 90 to help people decide what their roles in mission are and prepare for missionary work.

All audio and video tapes listed below may be ordered from 2100 Productions, P.O. Box 7895, Madison, Wisc. 53707, 1-800-828-2100.

Plenary Session Videos
$14.95 each
   Mary Fisher/Keren Everett: *God So Loved the World*
   Luis Bush/Dan Harrison
   George Otis, Jr./Anita Deyneka: *Branching Out*
   Ajith Fernando/Glandion Carney
   Paul Tokunaga: *Friends*
   Philemon Choi/Drama: *Cup A Coffee*/Caesar Molebatsi
   Ada Lum/Peter Kuzmic: *Students in World Mission*
   Isaac Canales/Drama: *. . . and the Spirit of God Dances!*/Global Issues Forum

Special Videos Shown at Urbana
$29.95 per tape
   Worldview Boutique: The Gospel in a Pluralist World (25 min)
   Picking up the Pieces: Broken People Serving a Broken World (25 min)
   Help and Hope: Good News for the Poor (25 min)
   God Is Building a City (14 min)

Urbana 90 Audio Cassettes
$6.95 each or $51.70 for the set
   #7186 "Colossians 1: Lordship of Christ," Luis Bush; "Colossians 2: The Uniqueness of Christ," Ajith Fernando.
   #7187 "Colossians 3: Spiritual Warfare and Holiness," Philemon Choi; "Colossians 4: Guidance," Isaac Canales.

#7188 "Jesus Christ: Hope of the World," Mary Fisher; "The Joy and Cost of Living the Gospel," Keren Everett; "Strongest in the Broken Places: Hope for the Hurting," Dan Harrison.

#7189 "Hope for Creative Access Countries," George Otis, Jr.; "Students in Creative Access Countries," Anita Deyneka; "Hope for the Cities," Glandion Carney.

#7190 "Hope for the Student World," Paul Tokunaga; "Hope for Racial Reconciliation in Mission," Caesar Molebatsi.

#7191 "Hope for Students of the World," Ada Lum; "Call to Commitment," Peter Kuzmic

#7192 "Student Congress on Global Issues," Glandion Carney/Bob Fryling; "Student Panel: My Response," Tana Clark.

Urbana Seminar Tapes
$6.95 each

#7195 "Multi-Ethnic Teams in Mission," Virgil Lee Amos

#7198 "Marriage and Ministry," Jerram Barrs

#7197 "Mission and Contextualization," Jerram Barrs

#7199 "Listening to the Voice of the Native American," Tony Begay

#7411 "Spirituality and Prayer," Jim Berney

#7416 "Reaching Disabled Persons for Christ," Joni Eareckson Tada

#7423 "Partnering for Radical Transformation of the Community," Caesar Molebatsi

#7424 "Ministry Among Mormons," Ken Mulholland

#7425 "Secular Employment for Creative Access Ministry," Dwight Nordstrom

#7427 "Witnessing Jesus' Way in a Pluralistic Society," Don Posterski

#7428 "How to Avoid Debt As You Go Through College," Mark Ritchie

#7434 "The New Believer's Entry into a Muslim World," Donna Smith

#7435 "Mission to Buddhists in a Shrinking World," Jim Stephens

#7439 "Spiritual Warfare in Mission," Jack Voelkel

#7440 "Your Church: A Sending Base for World Mission," Rev. Bill Waldrop

#7194 "Ministry to Homosexuals," Patricia Allan

#7196 "Reaching Hindu Families for Christ," Sakhi Athyal

#7418 "AIDS: Implications for World Mission," Debbie Dortzbach

#7419 "Involving Your Parents in Decision-Making," Stanley Inouye

#7420 "New Age: Search for Universal Religion," Eva and Joshi Jayaprakash

#7415 "Counselling in a Multi-Ethnic Context," Gerardo de Jesus-Lopez

#7421 "Women: Called to Minister," Dr. Catherine Kroeger

#7422 "Mission in Teams: Why and How?" Rev. Paul McKaughan

#7430 "Taking the Cities for God," Brenda Salter-McNeil/Rick Richardson

#7431 "Ministering Among Tribal Peoples," Linda Sheldon

#7433 "Global Revolutions and Christian Relief and Development," Amy Sherman

#7442 "Major Trends in World Mission," Dr. Ralph Winter

#7443 "Urban Trends: Consequences for Mission," Rev. Tom Wolfe
#7417 "People and Technology," Mary Fisher
#7426 "Changing Thinking in Changing Times," George Otis, Jr.
#7429 "Hope for Broken People," Dr. Dale Ryan
#7436 "Ecological Stewardship," Ruth Goring Stewart
#7437 "The Sanctity of Life," Dawn Swaby-Ellis, M.D.
#7193 "Leadership in the 21st Century," Gordon Aeschliman
#7413 "Multi-Ethnicity," Rev. Isaac Canales
#7414 "Urbanization," Rev. Glandion Carney
#7138 "Basic Human Needs," Dr. Bryan Truman
#7441 "Economic Justice," Jana Webb

Global Issues Bible Studies
$4.95 each

Produced for Urbana 90, this study series is designed to help you apply your faith to the challenging issues of today's world. Each guide contains an introduction to the topic and six Bible studies for individuals or groups. Available from Christian bookstores or InterVarsity Press, P.O. Box 1400, Downers Grove, Ill. 60515.

Basic Human Needs by Bryan Truman
Economic Justice by Jana L. Webb
Environmental Stewardship by Ruth Goring Stewart
Healing for Broken People by Dan Harrison
Leadership in the 21st Century by Gordon Aeschliman
Multi-Ethnicity by Isaac Canales
People and Technology by Mary Fisher
Sanctity of Life by E. Dawn Swaby-Ellis
Spiritual Conflict by Arthur F. Glasser
Urbanization by Glandion Carney
Voiceless People by Chuck Shelton